新编剑桥商务英语应试辅导用书

丛书主编 周之南
分册主编 张广林 杨 梅
副 主 编 王颖鹏 张 贺
张 伟 谷 珊

BEC

写作全攻略 高级

SUCCESS WITH BEC HIGHER

中国财经出版传媒集团
经济科学出版社
Economic Science Press

图书在版编目（CIP）数据

BEC 写作全攻略：高级/周之南主编；张广林，杨梅分册主编．—北京：经济科学出版社，2018.7（2019.6重印）

ISBN 978-7-5141-9521-7

Ⅰ.①B… Ⅱ.①周…②张…③杨… Ⅲ.①商务-英语-写作-自学参考资料 Ⅳ.①F7

中国版本图书馆 CIP 数据核字（2018）第 155255 号

责任编辑：孙怡虹　杨　洋
责任校对：杨晓莹
版式设计：齐　杰
责任印制：王世伟

BEC 写作全攻略（高级）
丛书主编　周之南
分册主编　张广林　杨　梅
经济科学出版社出版、发行　新华书店经销
社址：北京市海淀区阜成路甲 28 号　邮编：100142
总编部电话：010-88191217　发行部电话：010-88191522
网址：www.esp.com.cn
电子邮件：esp@esp.com.cn
天猫网店：经济科学出版社旗舰店
网址：http://jjkxcbs.tmall.com
北京密兴印刷有限公司印装
710×1000　16 开　12.25 印张　257000 字
2018 年 11 月第 1 版　2019 年 6 月第 2 次印刷
ISBN 978-7-5141-9521-7　定价：36.00 元

主编及主要编者简介

张广林：男，1962 年生，吉林大学公共外语教育学院教授，硕士生导师。长期从事跨文化交际和翻译理论与实践工作，担任吉林大学“外贸函电”“商务英语写作”“英美报刊选读”等多门课程主讲教师，并担任吉林大学考点商务英语口试考官。先后在国家核心刊物发表学术论文十余篇，已出版专（译）著5部，主持并完成国家级和省部级科研项目 4 项，编写国家级“十一五”规划教材 3 部。主要代表成果有：《博流英语》《下岗女工身份的社会语言学研究》等。

杨梅：女，1976 年生，吉林大学公共外语教育学院副教授。吉林大学外国语学院语言学硕士，英国阿伯丁大学语言学博士。研究方向：社会语言学、应用语言学、教师教育。

王颖鹏：女，1982 年生，吉林大学公共外语教育学院教师，吉林大学公共外语教育学院语言学硕士。主要从事吉林大学商务英语主干课程的讲授，并担任商务英语初、中级口试考官。多次指导学生参加“CCTV”杯全国英语演讲大赛以及全国大学生英语竞赛，并取得优异成绩。主要作品有《新要求大学泛听教程 1》。

张贺：女，1981 年生，吉林大学公共外语教育学院教师。剑桥商务英语考试考官。曾主讲吉林大学本科生商务英语第二学历《商务英语听力》。

张伟：男，1962 年生，副教授，吉林省长春市人，大学文化，获英国语言文学学士学位和比较文学与世界文学硕士学位，吉林大学公共外语教育学院教师。长期从事大学英语教学工作，具有丰富的教学经验。曾获 1988 ~ 1992 年度全国普通高校优秀教学成果省级二等奖一项。主要学术成果有论文《大学英语教学改革的尝试》《大学英语教学改革的实践与效果》。主要著作有《阅读与翻译实践》《新编大学英语四级技能训练》。译著有《牛津中学生英汉双解词典》。

谷珊：女，1969 年生，吉林大学公共外语教育学院副教授，长期从事语言文学以及翻译理论的研究和实践工作，担任吉林大学本科生的英语教学工作在各种刊物上发表论文 20 多篇主持并参与完成省级及校级科研项目 5 项，曾担任大学英语四级考试模拟试题解析的副主编，也担任过牛津学生英语双解词典的编译者。

前　言 Preface

众所周知，随着世界经济全球化步伐日益加快，中国经济与世界经济逐步接轨，国际商务往来日益频繁。语言作为一种必不可少的沟通桥梁，正在逐渐发挥它不可替代的重要作用。商务英语是一种在工作环境中使用的、世界通用的语言，适用于政府机关、事业单位、企业、商社等各种机构的日常公务和商贸活动。

商务英语证书（BEC）是教育部考试中心和英国剑桥大学考试委员会合作，根据公务或商务工作的实际需要，对考生在一般工作环境下和商务活动中使用英语的能力从听、说、读、写四个方面进行全面考查，对成绩合格者提供由英国剑桥大学考试委员会颁发的标准统一的成绩证书。由于其颁发机构的权威性，该证书在一百多个国家和地区的商业企业部门获得认可，成为证明证书持有者英语能力的首选，也是在所有举办该项考试的国家和地区求职的“通行证”。

《BEC写作全攻略》（初、中、高级）系列丛书则是专门为备考剑桥商务英语证书（Business English Certificate）而量身编写的配套用书。它有效地解决了国内考生在备考商务英语初、中、高级系列考试时，由于教材为国外原版引进，文化背景不同而导致的考生理解力有限的问题；同时它也满足了广大考生对写作进行专项辅导的要求，使商务英语的学习更加具体，解决了课堂教学兼顾听、说、读、写而导致的大而不精的问题。基于这些优势，本丛书重点体现了以下几个特点：

1. 分类详解，涵盖面广

BEC 考试分为初、中、高三个级别的考试。在每个级别的考试中，写作部分都包括两个任务：PART ONE 和 PART TWO。在同一级别的考试中，两个任务对写作的篇幅、类型和语言考察的侧重点都有明显不同的要求；在不同级别之间，相同的写作任务要求考生完成的写作篇幅、类型和文体也不相同。比如，在 BEC 初级的 PART ONE 中，考生应当完成一个简短的便条、留言条、备忘录或者电子邮件的写作；而在 BEC 高级的 PART ONE 中，考生则应依据图表写一个商务报告。因此，本丛书的每一册都分别详细地介绍了写作任务 1 和写作任务 2。并且在每个任务当中，又一一讲解了各种体裁的写作特点。

2. 立足真题，接近考试

由于是关于写作的针对性极强的书籍，因此在本丛书中必不可少地要出现大量写作练习题和写作范文。BEC 考试不同于其他国内英语语言类考试，它的写作会给考生模拟一个写作环境，比如简短的写作背景描述、图表、假定考生的作者身份或者写作角度等。因此，在本丛书中出现的写作题目要求大部分均来自历年的考试真题，或者由丛书作者依据剑桥大学考试委员会提供的考试手册要求，精心挑选国外商务或公务第一手素材编写而成。这样就使整套丛书更加接近 BEC 考试的真实环境和难度，使考生在最初备考时，就已经站在了和 BEC 相近的水平线上。有了明确的标准，才能保证最佳的学习质量。

3. 范文充足，讲解细致

本套丛书中出现的每个写作范例或练习，均配有相应的范文。这些范文大都是作者在教学第一线积累的学生作文，或者由作者亲自撰写，因此能鲜明地体现广大考生在写作当中出现的普遍性的问题，具有极强的代表性；由作者撰写的范文也均依据剑桥大学考试委员会提供的写作要求，具有鲜明的示范性。

此外，对于一些典型的范文，本丛书也做了细致的讲解。从词汇到篇章，从搭配到逻辑，从结构到思想，从体裁到文体，均做出了详细的说明。这也解决了许多年以来，广大考生没有系统地学习过英文篇章的撰写，写作时无从下手、考虑不周、表达不到位等诸多问题。

4. 应用性强，学以致用

国内学生多年的英语写作大都侧重于语法、词汇等语言层面上的学习，他们很少能将语言应用于真正意义上的工作或商务活动。更不要谈及用英语来创作正式、非正式的信函、撰写工作年度报告，商务分析、商务策划、工作备忘录等一系列非常具体的商务文章。因此，在校大中专生尽管学习了多年英语，但是一旦走上工作岗位，他们就会发觉自己学习的知识和实际工作之间有一定的距离。本丛书十分及时地解决了这个问题。丛书中提供了大量的商务和公务环境，并且配有充足的范例和讲解，这样一来，广大学生可以提前进行工作演练，为今后的实践应用积累足够的知识和经验，真正做到学以致用。

由于编者水平有限，编写时间仓促，不当和错误之处在所难免，欢迎广大读者批评指正。

编者

2018年5月

目 录 Contents

Week 1

了解BEC高级写作的要求

Day 1

BEC 考试的历史与 BEC 高级考试

1. 了解 BEC 考试的历史

剑桥商务英语证书（Cambridge Business English Certificate，BEC）考试，是英国剑桥大学考试委员会（University of Cambridge Local Examination Syndicate，UCLES）首先为我国的英语考生专门设计的一种英语水平考试，现已从中国推广到亚洲、欧洲、北美洲、南美洲、大洋洲等 60 多个国家。在中国，已有几十万考生参加了由剑桥 ESOL 考试部推出的剑桥商务英语证书考试（BEC）。

英国的剑桥大学（University of Cambridge）是一所世界闻名的高等学府。剑桥大学考试委员会是它的一个附属机构，创建于 1858 年。从 1863 年开始，该委员会开始为国外的考生设计考试，从 1913 年开始将英语为非母语国家的考试升级为以英语为外语的考试（English as a Foreign Language，EFL）。剑桥大学考试委员会是欧洲考试工作协会的创建者之一，该协会建立了欧洲统一的语言测试标准，BEC 考试就是根据上述标准设计的。

剑桥大学考试委员会正在全球范围内致力于建立一个测试商界雇员英语水平的统一标准，即让跨国公司及大型国内公司承认剑桥商务英语证书，BEC 证书已被许多非英语国家的大公司用作商务英语测试标准，以便公平地评估在真实商务环境下雇员的英语水平，使人力资源部门和培训部门能准确评估雇员商务英语的运用技能。它是根据英语为非母语国家人员进行国际商务活动的需要而设计的，主要为了适应我国的改革开放和国际经济贸易的日益频繁。该证书由于其颁发机构的权威性，被英国、英联邦各国及欧洲大多数国家的商业企业部门认可，成为确认证书持有者英语能力证明的首选，同时也是在所有举办该项考试的国家和地区求职的“通行证”。

为了适应改革开放的需要，教育部考试中心与剑桥大学考试委员会商定从

1993 年起，在中国合作举办剑桥商务英语考试。作为双方合作的第一个考试项目，双方协定首先举办剑桥商务英语证书考试（BEC）。根据中国的实际情况，剑桥大学聘请了许多 EFL 专家在剑桥商务英语证书考试系列中专门设计了较低和中上级别的两个考试，即商务英语证书考试（第一级）（Business English Certificate 1，BEC1）和商务英语证书考试（第二级）（Business English Certificate 2，BEC2），并将原有的国际商贸英语证书（Certificate in English for International Business and Trade，CEIBT）考试作为 BEC 考试第三级（BEC3），通过 BEC3 考试的考生将同时获得 CEIBT 证书，从而使得该考试与国际通用标准接轨。CEIBT 考试在欧美许多国家被广泛承认，是就业领域中最权威的英语能力证明。为进一步完善 BEC 系列考试，剑桥大学考试委员会在 1999 年开始对该项考试进行修订，并在 2002 年 3 月推出修订过的 BEC 考试，即 BEC PRELIMINARY（相当于原来的 BEC1）、BEC VANTAGE（相当于原来的 BEC2）、BEC HIGHER（相当于原来的 BEC3）。

根据中华人民共和国教育部考试中心与英国剑桥大学签订的协议，我国于 1993 年 11 月 21 日在北京、天津、上海、南京、广州、海口、福州七城市首次举行了剑桥商务英语证书（BEC）考试。自 1994 年起，这一考试已经在全国各省、直辖市、自治区开考，考试时间为每年的 5 月和 11 月。

2. 了解 BEC 高级考试

➤ 考试对象

一般来说，考生可根据自己的英语水平自由选择相应级别报考 BEC。报名不受年龄、性别、职业、地区、学历等限制，在剑桥商务英语考试官方报名网站实名注册后即可报名参加考试，在华工作的外籍人员和现役军人亦可持本人有效身份证件报名参加考试。

报考 BEC 高级的考生，英语水平一般略高于大学英语六级，相当于剑桥熟练英语证书考试（Certificate of Proficiency in English）。

➤ 考试流程

BEC 考试每年举行两次，时间为每年 5 月和 11 月。具体网上报名系统开通日期和各项步骤时间安排由官方报名网站发布。一般上午笔试，下午口试。口试进度慢的，延至第二天。考试地点为报名时选择考点，具体考场由各考点公布。BEC 考试顺序依次是阅读、写作、听力、口语。考试一般 8 点钟开始，最好提前 30 分钟到达。

考试答题卡由教育部考试中心汇集后寄英国剑桥大学考试委员会评卷。评出成绩后打印成绩通知单和成绩证书，寄至教育部考试中心后寄发各考点向考生颁发。

➤ 考试内容

BEC 高级考试分为阅读、写作、听力、口语共四个部分。阅读试卷和写作试卷是分开的两份试卷，之后的听力试卷也是单独试卷，听力考试有抄写答题卡的时间。口试部分是 2 个考官与 2 个或 3 个考生（如果考点考生是单数，最后一组考生是 3 个人）的面试形式。

BEC 高级考试的试题内容概述如下：

BEC Higher（高级）				
测试技巧	部分数量	小题数	时间	备注
阅读	6 部分	52 小题	60 分钟	
写作	2 部分	2 小题	70 分钟	
听力	3 部分	30 小题	40 分钟	40 分钟包括抄答题卡
口语	3 部分	不确定	16 分钟	

Day 2

BEC 高级考试写作概述及试卷结构

1. 概述

根据英国剑桥大学考试委员会提供的 Business English Certificates Handbook，我们可以清晰地了解到：

GENERAL DESCRIPTION

Paper format	The paper consists of two business related writing tasks in response to stimuli provided and for a given purpose and target reader.
Timing	1 hour 10 minutes.
No. of parts	There are two parts.
No. of tasks	Two (both are compulsory).
Task types	In Task One, candidates are required to write a short report. In Task Two, candidates are required to write either a report or a proposal or a piece of business correspondence.
Answer format	Candidates write their answers on the answer sheet.
Marks	Part 1 carries one third of the total marks available and Part 2 carries two thirds of the total marks available.

试卷形式：写作部分的试卷由两个与商务相关的写作任务组成，考生需要按照题目要求，完成一个给定写作背景下的特定的写作任务。

时间要求：1 小时 10 分钟。

组成部分：2 部分。

任务数量：2 个任务（均为必答题）。

任务类型：在任务一当中，考生需要写一个较短的商务报告。在任务二当中，考生会根据要求完成以下三种类型的写作当中的一篇即可：business report，business proposal，business correspondence。

作答形式：考生需要将答案写在答题纸上。

分值比例：第一部分的写作占写作总分数的1/3，第二部分的写作占写作总分数的2/3。

2. 试卷结构及测试重点

部分	功能	提示材料	题型	语域
1	能够描述或比较所给的示意图的数字，作出推断等	示意图和写作要求	短小的报告（形式可以是备忘录或者电子邮件）（120～140字）	中性 非正式
2	报告：描述、总结 建议书：描述、总结、推荐、劝说 函件：解释、道歉，消除疑虑、投诉等	写作要求。有时可能附有简短的正文，比如通知、广告等	学生可以从报告（形式可以是备忘录或者电子邮件）或建议（形式可以是备忘录或电子邮件）或者商务函件（形式可以是信件、传真或电子邮件）中选择一种（200～250字）	中性 非正式

BEC要求考生写两篇作文

第一篇　以示意图为基础的一篇短小报告

第二篇　以下内容之一（由考生选择）

- 一封商务函件：指就某个商务事宜写给公司以外的某个人（如顾客或者供应商），形式可以是信件、传真或电子邮件。
- 一份报告：报告将包括引言、正文和总结。报告可以通过备忘录或者电子邮件的方式来写。
- 一份建议：格式与报告相似，但又不同于报告。建议更倾向于对未来的关注，主要重点在于建议讨论的内容，形式可以是备忘录或电子邮件。

Day 3

BEC 高级写作评分原则

BEC 高级采用两套评分标准相结合的办法。一个是整体评分方法（General Impression Mark Scheme），另一个是基于特定任务的评分方法（Task - Specific Mark Scheme）。

整体评分方法重点关注于作文的内容，结构与连贯性，运用词汇的丰富性与灵活性，语法结构与使用的正确性。评分员会综合考虑以上这些方面给出一个总的印象分，分值一般都划分成五个等级，分别为 Band 1 ~ 5，其中 Band 5 为最高等级。BEC 高级的考生合格分数为 Band 3。

基于特定任务的评分方法则重点关注于每个部分中写作任务的完成情况。如果考生不能按要求完成特定写作任务，那么他的成绩必然会受到影响。

美式拼写和用法可以接受。第一部分的最后分值要转换为 10 分制的分数，第二部分分值要转换为 20 分制的分数。

以下是 BEC 高级写作中的整体评分方法的五个具体等级：

General Impression Mark Scheme

评分标准：第五级

Band 5：Full realization of the task set.

- All content points included.
- Controlled，natural use of language；minimal errors.
- Wide range of structure and vocabulary.
- Effectively organized，with appropriate use of cohesive devices.
- Register and format consistently appropriate.

Very positive effect on the reader.

这是写作最高的级别，相当于我们所说的“优秀”。大家可以看到该级别规定考生要能够全部完成答题要求；将所有的内容点都包括在内；语言规范、自然，错误最少；运用多样化的语言结构和词汇量；能够有效地组织，适当地使用前后呼应的方法；语域和格式完全适当；给读者的印象极佳。

评分标准：第四级

Band 4：Good realization of the task set.

- All major content points included；possibly minor omissions.
- Natural use of language；errors only when complex language is attempted.
- Good range of structure and vocabulary.
- Generally well organized，with attention paid to cohesion.
- Register and format on the whole appropriate.

Positive effect on the reader.

这是较高的一个级别，相当于我们所说的“良好”。这一级别要求考生能够较好完成答题要求；所有的内容要点已经包括在内，可能出现少量的遗漏；语言自然，但是在使用较复杂语言时，会出现错误；能够运用多样化的语言结构和丰富的词汇；总体的组织较好，且能够注意逻辑性；语域和格式总体来说使用恰当；给读者的印象很好。

评分标准：第三级

Band 3：Reasonable achievement of the task set.

- All major content points included；possibly minor omissions.
- Reasonable control，although a more ambitious attempt at the task may lead to a number of non-impeding errors.
- Adequate range of structure and vocabulary.
- Organization and cohesion is satisfactory.
- Register and format reasonable，although not entirely successful.

Satisfactory effect on the reader.

这是一个居中的等级，相当于我们所说的“合格”。这一级别中考生作文能基本达到题目要求；所有的主要内容点都已经包括进去，可能有少量的遗漏；语言比较规范，尽管在答题时更大胆地尝试了一些可能会导致不妨碍交流的错误；语言结构和词汇量适度；组织结构和逻辑性令人满意；语域和格式尽管不完全恰当，但是尚且能接受；给读者的印象较好。

评分标准：第二级

Band 2：Inadequate attempt at the task set.

- Some major content points omitted or inadequately dealt with; possibly some irrelevance.
- Errors sometimes obscure communication and are likely to be numerous.
- Limited range of structure and vocabulary; language is too elemental for this level.
- Content is not clearly organized.
- Unsuccessful attempt at appropriate register and format.

Negative effect on the reader.

这一级别已经属于不合格的范畴了，相当于“差”。考生的作文不能完全达到题目要求；遗漏一些主要的内容点或者处理得不适当，可能有些不切题；出现的错误影响交流并且可能错误较多；语言结构和词汇量掌握范围有限，这个水平的语言很初级；内容的组织条理不清晰；语域和格式运用不当；给读者的印象不佳。

评分标准：第一级

Band 1：Poor attempt at the task set.

- Notable content omissions and/or considerable irrelevance.
- Serious lack of control; frequent basic errors.
- Narrow range of structure and vocabulary.
- Lack of organization.
- Little attempt at appropriate register and format.

Very negative effect on the reader.

这个级别的作文“极差”，未能达到任务要求；有显著的内容遗漏和大量的内容不切题；语言严重不规范，经常出现基本错误；语言结构单一，词汇量贫乏；缺乏组织性，几乎没有使用适当的语域和格式；给读者的印象极差。

评分标准：第零级

Band 0：Achieves nothing. Either fewer than 25% of the required number of words or totally illegible or totally irrelevant.

该级别的作文什么任务也没有完成，字数少于所需字数的25%，或是完全看不懂，或是完全不切题。

Day 4

Question 1 写作样卷及不同级别的范文

1. Question 1 样卷

PART ONE

Question 1

- The bar chart below shows the cost of buying three different photocopiers, the cost of a warranty on each machine, and their expected running costs for the first two years.
- Using the information from the chart, write a short report comparing the costs for the three machines.
- Write 120 – 140 words on page 3.

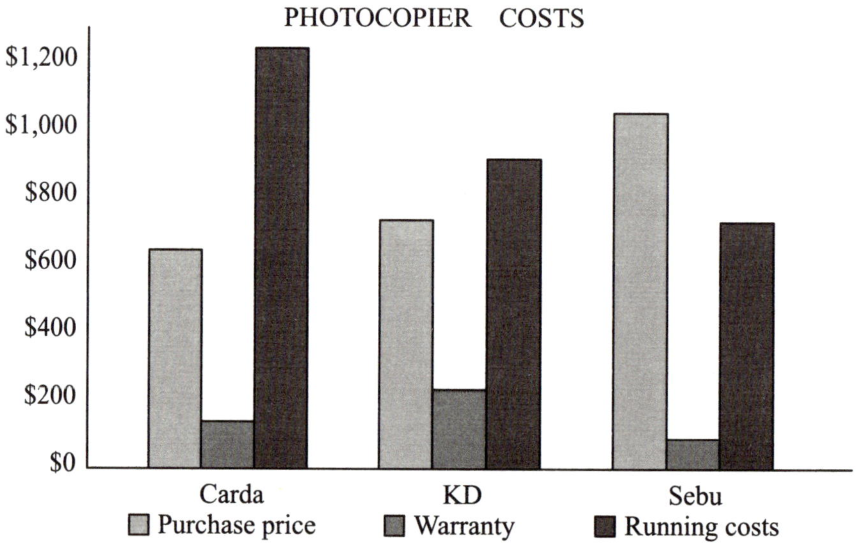

Expected total costs for initial 2-year period: Carda—$1,900
KD—$1,800
Sebu—$1,800

2. Question 1 范文 Report

➤ 五级作文

Of the three types of photocopiers, Carda, KD and Sebu, the purchase price of the Carda is the lowest. It is slightly more than $600 but its expected running cost for the first two years is the highest with its warranty cost at the mid-level of the three photocopiers.

In comparison, the purchase price of the KD is a little more than that of the Carda which is $700; whereas the expected running cost of the KD is much less than that of the Carda which is $1,200. However, the KD's warranty cost is the highest of the three at $200. In comparison, the Sebu's purchase price is the highest of the three, i.e. $1,000, but it costs consumers the least in warranty and running for the first two years.

What's more, the expected total cost of the Carda for the initial 2-year period is $1,900, more than that of both the Sebu and KD, $1,800. In conclusion, it would be advisable to buy the KD photocopier which is generally more advantageous in cost than its competitors.

> **批注：**此处表达略显模糊，"$1,800" 不能清晰地告诉读者究竟是指哪一家公司的成本。

Band 5

评语：该习作是一篇优秀的图表报告。首先能够利用图表中提供的信息，充分地完成写作任务，对三种机器的成本进行了详细的分析和比较。其次，该范文作者能对语言有一个良好的把握，使用语言自然得体，语言错误极少。例如，第一段的最后一句话，作者能够运用一个较为复杂的句式比较 Carda 和其他两种机器在成本上的差异和特点，这就体现了他对语言良好的把握能力。再次，文章的结构清晰，作者能够恰当地使用各种连接手法，例如："in comparison; whereas; however; but; what's more" 等。最后，语言正式，措辞中性严谨，体现出了商务报告在风格上的特点。例如，作者在习作中从来没有用到 "I; I think; I hope; you can find" 之类的涉及主观意愿的词汇。

➤ 四级作文

This report was compiled to present the data about the costs of buying three different photocopiers, the cost of a warranty on each machine, and their expected running costs for the first two years. The photocopiers being described are Carda, KS and Sebu.

Certainly the most expensive one is Carda as its total cost for initial 2-year period is $1,900. This includes running costs of $1,200 and cost of a warranty which is $100. The remaining part of costs – about 30% of the total costs – is the purchase price.

Total cost of both KD and Sebu photocopiers are equal, however, their particular ingredients differ. KD's warranty is the most pricey and costs $200 whereas Sebu's costs $70. Running costs of KD and Sebu photocopiers are $900 and $800, respectively. Taking into consideration purchase price, the most expensive one is Sebu which costs $1,000 whereas KD's is cheaper than Sebu by $200. Total costs for the 2-year period of these machines is $1,800.

I trust that the above data will be useful and helpful for the buyer to make the best possible choice.

批注 [1]: 应当为复数。

批注 [2]: 表意不准确。

批注 [3]: 语法错误："pricey"是形容词，表示昂贵的。它的最高级应当是加"est"。

批注 [4]: 主谓不一致。应当是"The total cost for the 2-year period of these machines is $1,800."。

评语：一篇比较好的习作。首先，从写作任务完成情况看，作者能够把所写的内容都包括在内，尽管不是完全正确。其次，在语言运用上我们能看出，有少量的语法错误，例如在形容词的比较级的使用，主谓单复数一致，以及表达的准确性等方面。但是作者对语言的把握能力还是比较好的，因为能够使用较复杂的句式，句子的结构种类较多，并且用词较丰富。此外，作者比较注意逻辑性。例如，第一段第一句话首先总体介绍了报告是关于三个产品的成本，于是在第二句话紧接着就进一步说明这三个产品分别是什么。最后，总体来说，这个文章也是一篇中性得体的商务报告，尽管在文章的最后运用了"I trust"这样的主观词汇。

➤ 三级作文

This report compares the costs of three photocopiers, called Carda, KD and Sebu.

Firstly, we will consider running costs. Far the highest is Carda's ($1,200) followed by KD's which is equal to $1,000 and the lowest one at the moment is Sebu's ($600). It also has the lowest warranty cost which is about $100. That is very close to the cost of Carda machine, which is just a bit higher ($630). But KD's cost is for about 100 percent higher than the mentioned two. If we look at purchase prices and start with the highest we firstly have to mention Carda. It's purchase price is $600, moving to KD with a price of about $700 and finish with the highest purchase price which is $1,200 and comes from Sebu.

If we analyse the facts I mentioned above we can calculate the expected total costs for initial 2-year period. Carda has the highest total cost which is $1,900, so it would be cheaper buying the other two, which both have a total price of $1,800.

批注[1]: 不完整的后置定语，应当改为定语从句。

批注[2]: 指代不清。

批注[3]: 多余的表达。

批注[4]: 语序错误。

批注[5]: "It's" 语法错误，应为 "Its"；这个句子表意混乱，句子中的主语不一致，且句子中主谓语之间的逻辑关系不清晰。

批注[6]: "buying the other two" 的逻辑主语不明朗而且表意不清。

评语：该习作属于我们汉语所说的"合格"。首先，基本上完成了写作任务，但是有些内容有所遗漏。例如在第一段就没有说明成本包括三个方面。其次，我们能看出作者的语言运用能力一般，因为在描述某种产品的某个特定成本是多少钱时，作者不能够用一个完整的句子或从句来表达，他大多都用括号标注的方法，这体现出了作者对语言的掌控和表达还不是很自如。但是整个文章中仍然能出现较复杂的句式，例如定语从句等，并且能够实现不同事物的比较。再次，在结构上，作者的表达有条理，能使用"firstly，also"等体现事物的内在关联。最后，从语言风格上看，文章中出现了很多口语化的词汇，例如："a bit；if we look at；we will"等，和题目要求不太一致，但是尚能被读者接受。

➤ 二级作文

The upper is the comparison of the costs of 3 different photocopiers, including the purchase price, warranty costs and expected running costs for initial 2-year. From that, we can see Carda gets the higest expected total costs of $1,900. The others, KD and Sebu are likely the same reaching $1,800.

The reason why Carda is the most expensive is due to its running costs, which covers more than 60 percent in the expected total cost. While KD and Sebu cost lower than that, no more than $1,000. In which Sebu's cost in running cost is only $800 around. But Sebu's buying cost the higest over $1,000. At the same time, Carda costs only $600, KD $700 or so. As to the cost of a warranty on them, KD is more than $200, Carda $120 and Sebu less than £100.

批注 [1]: 表意不清，应当是“The upper chart”。

批注 [2]: 这种表达只能做定语，应当改为“two years”。

批注 [3]: 应当改为后置定语补充说明“cost”。

批注 [4]: 用词错误，应当是“almost”。

批注 [5]: 表述错误，应当为“why Carda's total cost is the highest”。

批注 [6]: 不完整的句式。

批注 [7]: 应当添加“is”。

批注 [8]: 应当用定语从句。

批注 [9]: 货币单位错误。

评语：该习作不能顺利地完成写作任务。通篇文章的语言错误过多，例如：“the upper; in which Sebu's cost in running cost is only $800”等，导致不能清晰地表达所要表述的内容，造成了读者理解上的障碍。并且在文章的结构上，我们看不到“总分总”“第一、第二、第三”等特征，这样导致读者很难将文章内容进行分类或者找不出文章的重点。通篇给读者的印象比较差。

Day 5

Question 2 写作样卷及不同级别的范文

1. Question 2 样卷

PART TWO

Questions 2 – 4

- Write an answer to one of the questions 2 – 4 in this part.
- Write 200 – 250 words on pages 5 and 6.
- Write the question number in the box at the top of page 5.

Question 2

- Your manager is keen to introduce new practices into your company. He has asked you to write a report which includes details of two practices from another company which you would suggest adopting in your own company.
- Write the report for your manager, including the following information:
  · what you admire about the other company.
  · which two of its practices you would adopt.
  · why your company would benefit from them.

2. Question 2 范文 Report

➤ 四级作文

The report sets out to describe the most attractive features of the Olive Garden chain restaurants' Staff Management policies and to suggest introduction of several

批注[1]: 表述略显模糊，应当加"'s"。

items into the restaurant department of the Hinton Firs hotel. The presented information has been obtained during the Assistant Manager's visit to the former company.

It was found that one of the American chain restaurants is exposed to an exceptionately innovative management that has recently developed a new policy in order to maintain high standards in all aspects of the service provided to their guests. It seems that two of its recently introduced practices may well be borrowed and implemented in our business.

Firstly, all the waiting staff are exposed to a check-up before starting their lunch and dinner shifts so as to ensure maintenance of hygene and compliance with the company's dress code.

Secondly, the evening briefings conducted on a regular basis in order to inform the staff about the basic changes in the menu and wine supplies have proved effective, and therefore could be applied in our restaurant department as well.

批注[2]: 应当是被动语态"have been proved"。

It is clear that a successful introduction of the two procedures is sure to reflect on the quality of such service in issues of the waiting staff's better awareness and an improvement in the hotel's image.

评语：这是一篇比较好的习作，能够完成题目要求的所有写作任务。语言使用比较自然，而且词汇丰富。尽管文章中有表述不够清晰或极少的表达错误，但是作者能用到例如"set out to; obtain; be exposed to; it seems that"等使表达具体，能够顺利完成写作任务的短语、词汇和句式等，并且文章中的句子结构丰富，能灵活运用多种句式。再者，这篇文章的结构清晰、条理清楚。作者能够较合理地规划段落，并恰当地使用一些连接手段。例如："firstly; secondly"等。此外，从语言风格上看，整篇文章正式得体，体现了商务报告严谨规范的特点。

➤ 二级作文

The purpose of this report is to established which practices should we accept in our company from company "Johnson". The company Johnson is well respected company in Europe. They own their success to inovation and team work. This is a well organized company with 300 employees. All their employees know what is expected from them. The company is devided in to departaments; production, finances, marketing and salles.

They have strict behaviour rules which includes non smoking and clothing polici. Inspite of this strict rules there is an open-level management. Every two weeks the main director receves employees that come with new ideas and they are reworded if the idea is accepted. Johnson has also an complain service in which pesonel can come to express their dissatisfaction.

In our company I would strongly sugest that we also adopt open-level management where we could widen our prospectives and get new ideas.

I also reccomend complain service center where we could find out how to motivate our staff.

批注[1]: 语法错误，应当是"establish"。

批注[2]: 拼写错误，应当是"innovation"。

批注[3]: 拼写错误，应当是"divided"。

批注[4]: 拼写错误，应当是"departments"。

批注[5]: 拼写错误，应当是"sales"。

批注[6]: 语法错误，主谓单复数不一致。

批注[7]: 拼写错误，应当是"policy"。

批注[8]: 单复数不一致，"these"。

批注[9]: 拼写错误，应当是"receives"。

批注[10]: 冠词使用错误，"a"。

批注[11]: 拼写错误，应当是"personnel"。

批注[12]:后边应当有逗号。

批注[13]: 拼写错误，应当是"suggest"。

批注[14]: 没有"s"。

批注[15]: 表意模糊，且拼写错误。

评语：该习作不能恰当地完成写作任务，虽然它包含了主要的内容，但是也遗漏了大量信息。并且语言错误极其多，尤其是拼写错误和语法错误等。在复杂句的使用中，普遍都有表达模糊的问题，而且语言风格口语化，不能恰当地展开论述，给读者的阅读和理解带来了麻烦。

Day 6

Question 3 写作样卷及不同级别的范文

1. Question 3 样卷

PART TWO

Questions 2 – 4

- Write an answer to one of the questions 2 – 4 in this part.
- Write 200 – 250 words on pages 5 and 6.
- Write the question number in the box at the top of page 5.

Question 3

- Your company has employed an outside consultant to organise an exhibition of your products, to be held next month. His work is unsatisfactory, and your boss has now decided that you should take over full responsibility instead. Your boss has asked you to write to the consultant to explain why he has been replaced.
- Write the letter to the consultant:
  - giving two reasons why he has been replaced.
  - telling him he will be paid for this work.
  - asking him to brief you on the current situation.

2. Question 3 范文 Letter

➤ 四级作文

Dear Mr. Jones,

My name is Svenja Pietzonka. I am an employee of a company Ardo, where you were employed. I have been given this unpleasant job of contacting you and explaining why you have been replaced. Another reason for writing you is to inform you that I will take over your responsibility and to ask for your help.

批注[1]: 语法错误，应当为“writing to you”。

The reasons for your replacement are, as you can assume, that you didn't know our products well enough. You obviously didn't quite understand which are the features of our products that attract potential customers and what our marketing strategies are. This led to the lack of ideas that you had. We know that you introduced a few ideas, but we think you would agree that none were satisfactory. We hope that you understand why we decided so.

批注[2]: 语法错误，应当为“is”。

批注[3]: 表意模糊。

We confess that your failure to succeed is also our fault. We should have introduced you to our products better and we should have let you know what the objectives of our company are and which market strategies we use to achieve them. Taking all these factors into account, we agreed that we should pay you the work you have done.

批注[4]: 逻辑错误，应当为“introduced our products to you”。

批注[5]: 重复。

I would like to ask you if you could brief me on the current situation. You probably know that it is extremely hard to start a project when someone was working on it before you, so I honestly hope that you will be prepared to assist me with your help.

批注[6]: 多余。

I am looking forward to hearing from you soon.

Yours sincerely,

Svenja Pietzonka

评语：该习作能够比较出色地完成写作任务，并且几乎涵盖了题目要求中的所有内容。从语气和口吻上看，这封商务信函符合题目所设置的背景要求，能够正确地使用敬语、结束语等。在信函的开头能够开门见山，正文中使用礼貌的表达，例如：“we hope that; we should have introduced; I would like to”等结构。从语言上看，作者使用词汇较丰富，但是整体上能使用较复杂的句式，例如复合句，独立结构，虚拟语气等。而且通篇的布局合理，第一段介绍写作目的，第二、第三、第四段就按照第一段说明的写作目的来一一展开。但是我们也能发现文章有少量的语法错误和表达不清晰或冗长等毛病。

➤ 二级作文

Dear sir,

Thank you for the work you have done to organise an exhibition. Most things are kept in order in the stage of the whole process and your job is confirmed and phrased by our boss to some extent. However, there still remains some shortcomings. As is known to all, you are a very excellent consultant in many respects. You have lots of experience in advising. But that it is based on outside conditions does not fit us very much. The policies, the strategies seem a bit different from what we own. And that causes some barriers among our people. So with the development of the process, the organising work may not be well done. To avoid such shortcomings, we may appreciate someone with local experience in the next stage of the process. Probably he will be helpful to the co-operative work, and accepted by the inside ones. He may not be as creative as you but somehow suits the situation now.

We will pay you according to your creative work and helpful advice and you will be thanked for your favour in our company.

As I will take your place and hopefully I intend to get some help from you. If you could brief the work on the current situation, I shall be very grateful. Thank you very much again.

Look forward to hearing from you.

Regards.

Jessica Choi

Company Advisor

批注 [1]: 表达不清晰。

批注 [2]: 拼写错误，应当为“praised”。

批注 [3]: 表意不清。

批注 [4]: 中间用and连接。

批注 [5]: 表意不清。

批注 [6]: 用词不准，“internal”。

批注 [7]: 表意不清。

评语：该文章尽管包括了全部写作内容，并且格式和语言风格符合题目预设的商务信函的要求，但是我们不难发现，作者语言运用能力较差。使用了大量超出自己使用能力的词汇，导致出现了过多的表达和语法错误。例如："phrased；shortcomings；inside"等词汇非但没能实现预想的表达效果，反而给读者造成了理解上的障碍，并且很多句子表意不清，给读者造成了不知所云的感觉，有时甚至需要读者去猜测部分句子的意思。

Day 7

Question 4 写作样卷及不同级别的范文

1. Question 4 样卷

PART TWO

Questions 2 – 4

- Write an answer to one of the questions 2 – 4 in this part.
- Write 200 – 250 words on pages 5 and 6.
- Write the question number in the box at the top of page 5.

Question 4

- Your company has decided to conduct an investigation into the possibility of increasing the number of ways in which technology is used throughout the organisation. You have been asked to write a proposal concerning the use of technology in your department for the Managing Director.
- Write your proposal, including the following:
  - a brief outline of the current uses of technology in your department.
  - a description of what technological improvements could be made.
  - an explanation of the benefits these changes might bring.
  - recommendations for the kind of training that would be necessary.

2. Question 4 范文 Proposal

➤ 五级作文

Purpose

As requested, the purpose of this proposal is to describe and analyse the possible use of technology in the Marketing Department.

Current use of technology

Up to now the members of our department have taken advantage of technological equipment i. e. computers, in order to launch our products most successfully. Not only have we arranged promotional and advertising campaigns but we have also conducted market research via the internet so as to meet our consumers' growing demands.

Technological Improvements

In our work we have used computer software and hardware which has already become obsolete and urgently needs modernisation. Therefore, the purchase of up-to-date programmes and equipment is of prime importance.

Benefits

There is no denying that these improvements will bring vast profits to the company. Our team will be able to work faster, more effectively and make greater use of technological innovations. Moreover, our company will be more likely to easily overcome fierce competition in the market.

Training

It seems obvious that our staff does not possess the knowledge of how to use new software. Thus, training on the use of modern programmes would be recommended as necessary.

Conclusion

To sum up, it seems obvious that the introduction of new technology into the Marketing Department will enable the company to gain huge profits. Our position in the market will be strengthened.

评语：这是一篇十分优秀的习作。作者出色地完成了题目规定的写作任务，涵盖了所有内容。这篇习作首先给读者的印象就是结构清晰，完全符合商务建议的格式要求，例如：每一个部分的标题都使用名词或名词性短语。此外，作者的语言精练，表达清楚、到位。例如在第一部分中，作者介绍了写作目的仅用了一个句子，并且能够使用“describe”和“analyse”精确地定位文章接下来要写的主要内容。而且在通篇中我们能看到很多精彩的表达，例如：“have taken advantage of; in order to; there is no denying that; it seems obvious that; not only...but...”等结构，并且句式十分丰富灵活，能够自如地运用长短句、简单句和复合句等。再者，作者运用了大量的连接手段，体现出了文章严谨的逻辑和谋篇布局，例如：“therefore; moreover; to sum up”等。最后我们不难发现，这篇商务建议的语气和口吻也十分的正式和中性，丝毫看不出个人的主观态度等，这也能体现出作者是经过缜密分析做出的建议，而非主观意愿的随意表达。

➤ 三级作文

The purpose of the proposal is to explain why our Design Department need to improve technology in our department regarding the introduction of more portable PCs and laser printers, and recommend some necessary training.

批注[1]: 语法错误，“needs”。

As designers in Design Department, it is our routine job to design our product consistent with the requirement of our clients. With the expanding of our company, we receive more orders. Most of our equipment: fax machines, color boards, etc. perform less help to us with our heavy workload. Our efficiency was affected.

批注[2]: 应当为复数。

批注[3]: 应当为复数。

批注[4]: 应当为复数。

There is therefore an urgent need for us to buy some more computers. Because, so many things can be done by computers, you can choose colors, textile types, etc. on them. And it is amazing to see the whole process on computer. Furthermore it is faster and quality is improved too.

批注[1]: 用词不准，应当为“via”表示“通过”。

批注[2]: 后边应当有逗号。

批注[3]: 表述不清，不知是在指什么东西的质量。

We usually attend some seminars or shows abroad. And we feel it is very inconvenient to take many design papers, and documents with us, and sometimes they are in a mess.

批注[4]: 改为转折更恰当。

So I think we should buy some portable computers for our designers, if possible. Besides that, it is paramount for us to get the latest information from all over the world. We could get them through internet with our portable computers anywhere, any time.

As our routine work has little connection with computers and internet, most of us can't use them freely. So it is necessary for us to bring in some training courses for computers and internet.

批注 [5]: 用词错误，应当是："Besides"，或者"Beside that"。

批注 [6]: 前后不一致，前边说急需电脑，这里又说电脑和工作无关。

批注 [7]: 应当是 "about"。

评语：该习作能够较合理地完成写作任务。首先，将所有主要内容包括在内，尽管有一些次重要的内容有所遗漏。其次，文章的结构组织比较合理，能运用段落的划分来一一完成不同的写作任务。最后，作者使用了一些超出自己能力的表达以期实现写作任务要求，但是我们发现这导致了诸多的结构错误和词汇使用错误。但是整体上看，这些错误不影响读者的理解。

Week 2

图表与商务报告的写作攻略

Day 1

图表描述类题型特点

1. 写作任务解析

这部分的写作在一开始，就有一个写作要求，同时会配有一个图表。要求考生写一篇 120 ~ 140 字的报告表述趋势和走向。该题型测试考生简洁、明快的写作技能、要求考生分析对比以曲线图、条形图、圆形分析图等形式表现的直观信息。考生需要应用表达趋势的得体语言，简洁地进行表述，避免超过规定的字数。

题目要求：

- 完成题目要求的能力指：完成要求的全部写作任务。只有在充分、得体地达到题目要求时，才有可能得到满分。
- 作文篇幅要控制在规定的字数内。如果作文字数低于规定的字数，说明未能充分完成题目要求；如果高于规定字数，则说明你的作文可能包含了多余的内容。

2. 语言表达特点

➤ 常见的图表种类

(1) 表格（table）。表格是提供信息最直接的方法，它能把收集到的信息，用行（row）和列（column）的组合系统排列出来，有助于人们在了解原始材料的基础上，做出归纳和判断。请看以下表格：

Purchased Equipments(June,2006)			
Item Num#	Item Picture	Item Description	Price
		Shipping Handling,Installation,etc.	Expense
1.		IBM Clone Computer	$400.00
		Shipping Handling,Installation,etc	$20.00
2.		1GB RAM Module for Computer	$50.00
		Shipping Handling,Installation,etc.	$14.00
Purchased Equipments(June,2006)			

（2）饼状图（pie chart）。饼状图适用于一个整体的各个组成部分之间的相互比较。一个大圆代表 100%，各个大小不一的扇形分别代表各个组成部分占整体的百分比。饼状图最大的优点就是能帮助人们认识到各个部分在整体中所占的份额大小。请看下图：

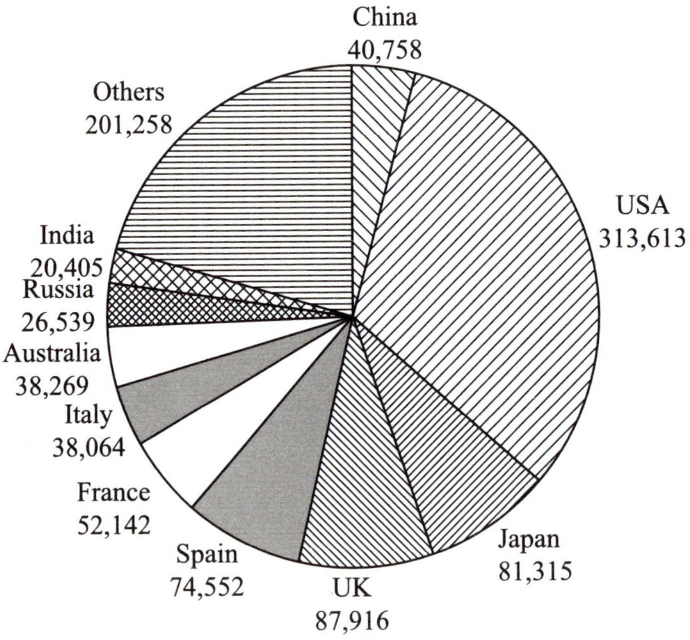

（3）柱状图（bar chart）。柱状图分为水平柱状图和垂直柱状图两种，他们是利用柱体的长短变化，比较一个或几个整体各个部分之间相对数量的变化，从而帮助人们直观地了解各个部分之间的数量之比。请看下图：

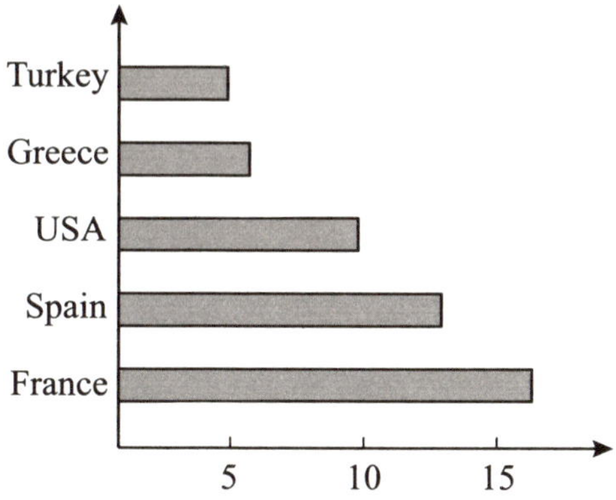

（4）曲线图（line chart）。曲线图借助于坐标系统，横轴反映时间的变化，纵轴反映数量的变化，用直线或者曲线来表示时间和数量之间的二维变化关系。

它特别适用于在某一特定的时期内一系列连线的数据变化。在曲线图中如果需要同时呈现一种以上的情形，可以采用不同的线条，比如：实线、虚线、点线等。或者可以采用不同的颜色来描绘不同的线条，以将它们区分开来。请看下图：

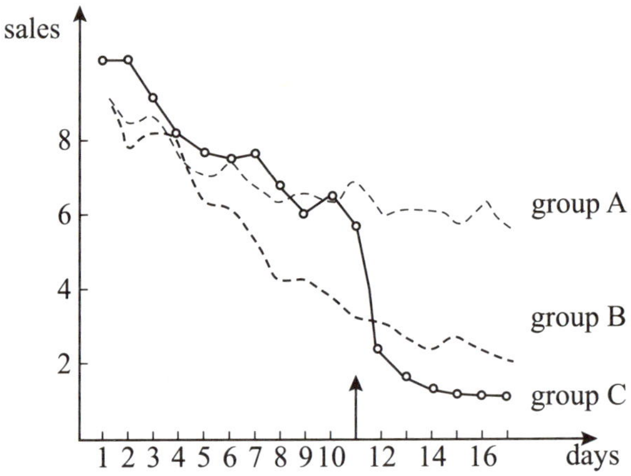

➤ 图表描述实例

（1）平稳趋势。

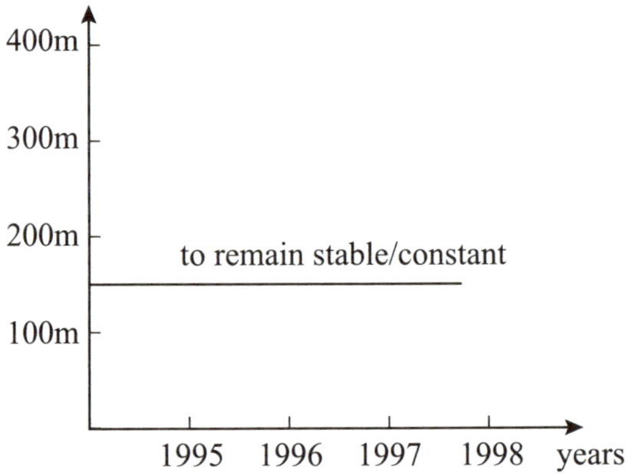

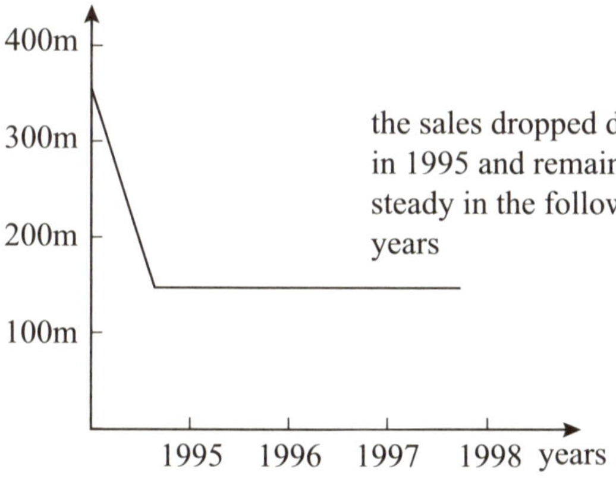
400m
300m
200m
100m
the sales dropped down in 1995 and remained steady in the following years
1995
1996
1997
1998
years

（2）上升趋势。

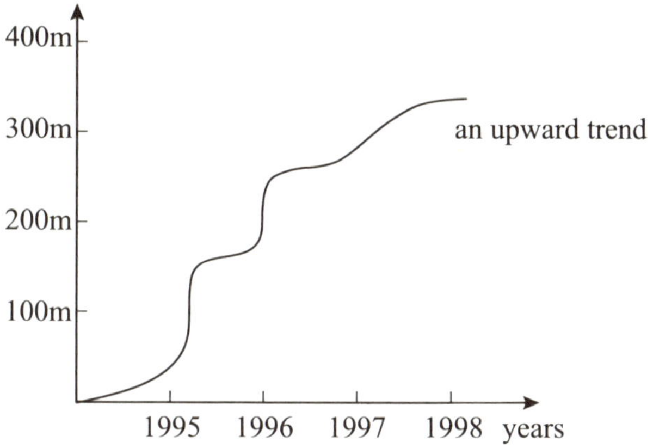
400m
300m
200m
100m
an upward trend
1995
1996
1997
1998
years

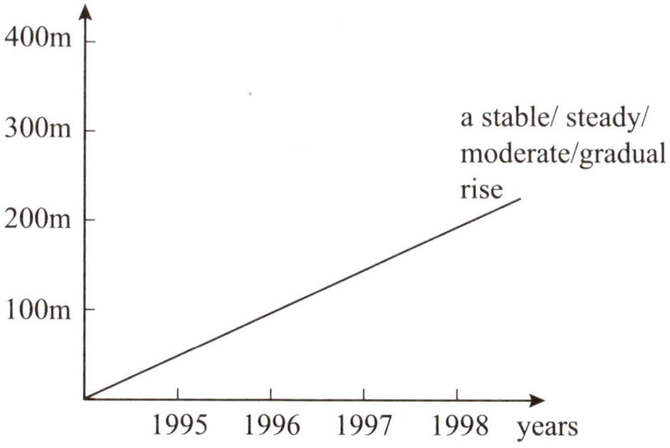
400m
300m
200m
100m
a stable/ steady/ moderate/gradual rise
1995
1996
1997
1998
years

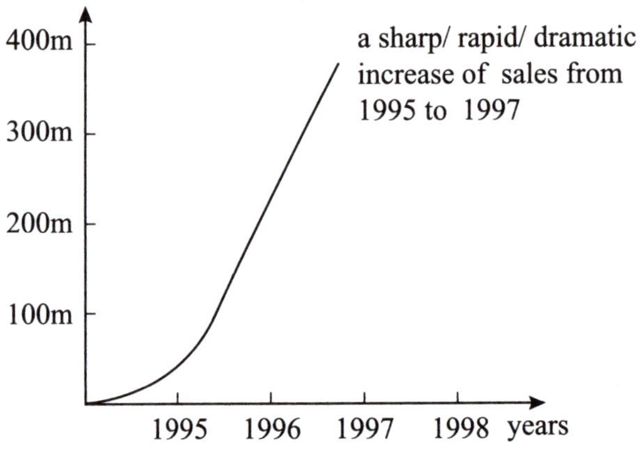
400m
300m
200m
100m
a sharp/ rapid/ dramatic increase of sales from 1995 to 1997
1995
1996
1997
1998
years

（3）下降趋势。

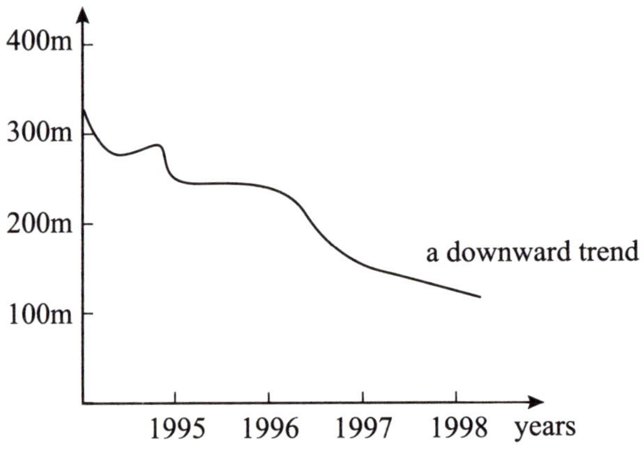
400m
300m
200m
100m
a downward trend
1995
1996
1997
1998
years

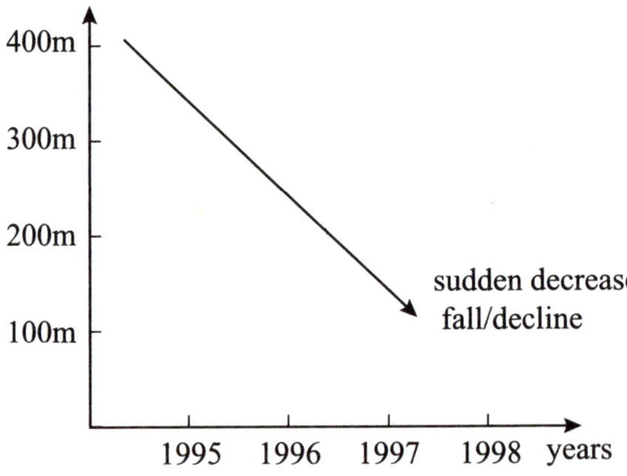
400m
300m
200m
100m
sudden decrease/ fall/decline
1995
1996
1997
1998
years

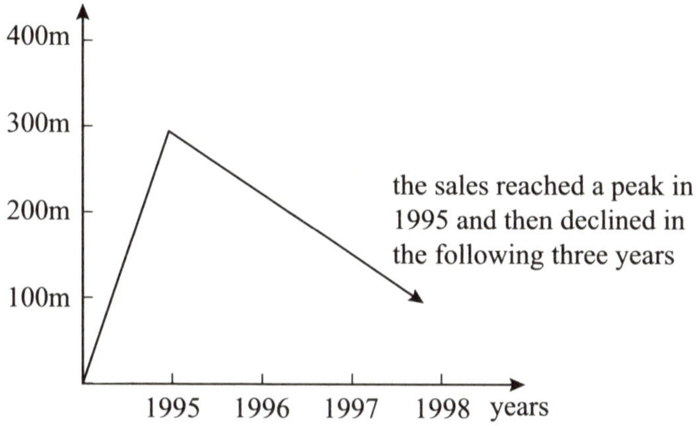
400m
300m
200m
100m
the sales reached a peak in 1995 and then declined in the following three years
1995
1996
1997
1998
years

（4）不稳定趋势。

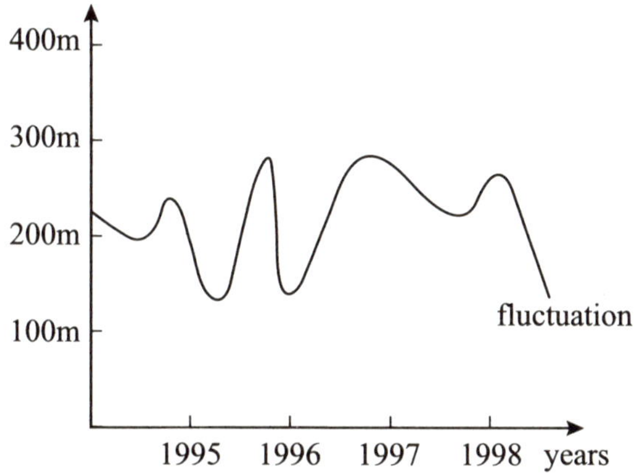
400m
300m
200m
100m
fluctuation
1995
1996
1997
1998
years

Day 2

图表描述的常用表达

1. 各种图表的说法

- 泛指一份数据图表：a data graph/chart/diagram/illustration/table
- 饼图：pie chart
- 直方图或柱形图：bar chart/histogram
- 趋势曲线图：line chart/curve diagram
- 表格图：table
- 流程图或过程图：flow chart/sequence diagram
- 程序图：processing/procedures diagram

2. 常用的描述用法

- The table/chart diagram/graph shows (that)
- According to the table/chart diagram/graph
- As (is) shown in the table/chart diagram/graph
- As can be seen from the table/chart/diagram/graph/figures
- figures/statistics shows (that) …
- It can be seen from the figures/statistics
- We can see from the figures/statistics
- It is clear from the figures/statistics
- It is apparent from the figures/statistics
- table/chart/diagram/graph figures (that) …
- table/chart/diagram/graph shows/describes/illustrates how…

3. 图表中的数据（Data）具体表达法

- 数据（Data）在某一个时间段固定不变：fixed in time
- 在一系列的时间段中转变：changes over time
- 持续变化的 data 在不同情况下：

  增加：increase/raise/rise/go up…

  减少：decrease/grow down/drop/fall…

  波动：fluctuate/rebound/undulate/wave…

  稳定：remain stable/stabilize/level off…
- 最常用的两种表达法：

  动词 + 副词形式（Verb + Adverb form）

  形容词 + 名词形式（Adjective + Noun form）

4. 表示数据变化的单词或者词组

- rapid/rapidly　迅速的，飞快的，险峻的
- dramatic/dramatically　戏剧性的，生动的
- significant/significantly　有意义的，重大的，重要的
- sharp/sharply　锐利的，明显的，急剧的
- steep/steeply　急剧升降的
- steady/steadily　稳固的，坚定不移的
- gradual/gradually　渐进的，逐渐的
- slow/slowly　缓慢的，不活跃的
- slight/slightly　轻微的、略微地
- stable/stably　稳定的

5. 其他在描述中的常用到的词

- significant changes　图中一些较大变化

- noticeable trend　明显趋势
- during the same period　在同一时期
- grow/grew　增长
- distribute　分布，区别
- unequally　不相等地
- in the case of　在……的情况下
- in terms of/in respect of/regarding　在……方面
- in contrast　相反，大不相同
- government policy　政府政策
- market forces　市场力量
- measure　n. 尺寸，方法，措施 v. 估量，调节
- forecast　n. 先见，预见 v. 预测

Day 3

图表描述类题型例文分析点评

1. 样题

Part One

- The graph below shows sales for two companies between 1995 – 1999.
- Using information from the graph, write a short report describing and comparing the performance of the two companies during this period.
- Write 120 – 140 words on your Answer Sheet.

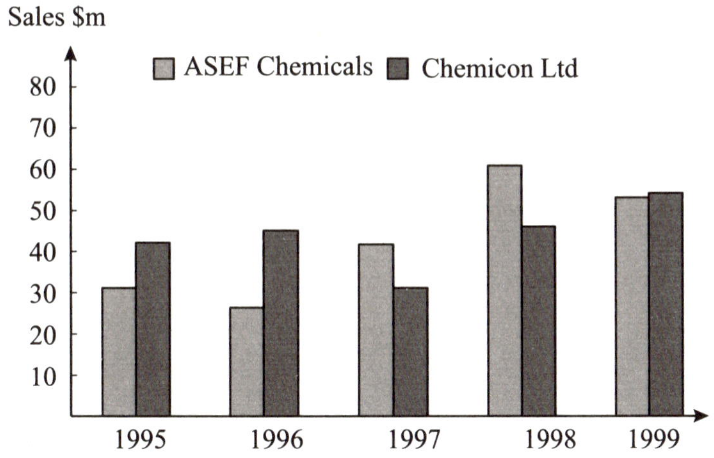

2. 习作例文

In 1995, ASEF Chemicals had the sales of about $30m and then in the next year, that was 1996, the sales declined down to $20m. In 1997, the sales were more than that of 1996, more than $40m. But in the next year, the sales increased more quickly than in 1995, 1996 and 1997, which was about $60m. But in 1999, sales were not so satisfied, it went down to $50m and this was the second largest sales from 1995 to 1999.

However, the sales in Chemicon Ltd were different from that in ASEF Chemicals. In 1995, the sales were about $40m, which was about $10m more than ASEF. The sales in 1995, 1996 and 1998 are almost the same, about $40m. But the sales in 1997 and 1998 in Chemicon Ltd were much less than that in ASEF. The two companies had almost the same sales in 1999, and that was the highest in Chemicon Ltd. Generally, despite an decrease in 1997, the sales in Chemicon were mostly stable during the five years. However, the sales in ASEF showed a rising tendency and reached its summit in 1998.

3. 例文点评

该作文未能充分达到题目的要求，共 189 字，远远超过了规定的字数。另外，考生在第一段一直都在流水账式地记录一个公司的业绩状况，直到第二段才开始对两家公司的业绩进行比较。因此，由于时间有限，字数有限，切记要描述总体趋势。如果句子短一些，用词简洁一些，减少一些重复，去掉多余的词，多使用一些省略表达和指示词，该作文会变得简洁许多。

在该作文修改过程中，我们应当从以下几个方面着手：

（1）表达要准确。在比较两个事物时，要注意比较的主体应当是具有相同性质的。比如说："In 1995, the sales were about $40m, which was about $10m more than ASEF"。在这一句中我们不难看出来，考生是想比较两个公司的销售情况，但写出的这个句子则是用甲公司的"销售"和乙公司本身相比较，我们知道，"销售"和"公司"是两个不相同的主体，它们没有可比性。此外，"satisfied"就应当换成"satisfying"。

（2）累赘冗长现象。考生应学会去掉不必要的词或者信息，例如："and then in the next year, that was 1996"，中的"that was 1996"应当去掉。此外，考生还应该学会用简短的表达替代冗长的表达，例如："But in 1999, sales were not so satisfied, it went down to \$50m and this was the second largest sales from 1995 to 1999"。可以改写成为"In 1999 sales were not so satisfying, but \$50m was still the second largest sales from 1995 to 1999"。句子的准确程度受句子长度的影响。长句容易引起混乱，考生应该检查自己所写的长句是否表达清晰；在商务写作中，应当牢记 KISS 原则：即"keep it short and simple"（写短小简单的句子）。

（3）指示词。诸如"it, they, which"等指示词可以帮助考生在写作时避免单词、句子甚至是段落的重复，使行文简洁。但值得注意的是，考生要保证他们使用的代词指代明确。

（4）衔接。在这篇习作中，我们会发现衔接用法诸如："however, but, whereas, on the whole, in contrast"等出现得比较少，这样就会使每个句子之间的逻辑关联不是很强烈，让读者觉得读起来比较生硬。

（5）重复。任何没有理由的信息重复都应该删除。通过使用指示词和省略手段可以避免单词和短语的重复。

4. 例文修改稿

Despite the fact that sales at both ASEF Chemicals and Chemicon Ltd experienced a number of fluctuations over the period 1995 – 1999, both companies showed a general upward trend in general.

At the beginning of the period ASEF sales stood at just over \$ 30m. They experienced a fall the following year, before picking up again in 1997 and reaching a peak of \$60m in 1998. Sales fell again slightly the following year but remained higher than their 1997 level. Chemicon sales exceeded those of ASEF in 1995 (\$ 42m compared to \$31m). Despite experiencing a fall in 1997, the overall trend was a slight rise over the four years period. Both companies ended 1999 with turnover of around \$50 with Chemicon outselling ASEF for the first time since 1996.

Day 4

商务报告类题型特点

1. 写作任务解析

商务报告类的作文会同时出现在 BEC 考试的写作第一题和第二题中。在第一题的写作中，一般都会要求考生根据图表写一篇字数在 120 ~ 140 字的简短的商务报告，关于这部分的内容，我们已经在之前做了详尽的说明。

在写作任务的第二题中，考生也往往会遇到要求“写一篇商务报告”这样的题目。这一部分就要求考生写一个较为正式、篇幅较长的报告，一般字数在 200 ~ 250 字，需要用 40 ~ 50 分钟来完成这部分的任务。这部分的题目要求有两点：一般第一点是给出一个写作环境，并且陈述要完成报告的一个具体背景；第二点中会列出在这个报告应当写什么，写给谁，以及具体包括哪些内容（一般为 3 ~ 4 点）。考生需要设身处地地站在考试方要求的写作背景下，按照要求具体的完成这个写作任务。

考生在正式写作之前，最好是先勾勒一个写作提纲，并在提纲中简洁地标明每部分应当包括的内容。最好的办法是按照写作任务要求，逐一写出它规定应当包括的 3 ~ 4 点。在这里我们不建议大家调整这几点的顺序，因为一旦遗忘了一点，就会造成相应的失分。并且在具体的写作中，我们还建议大家在写商务报告时，给这个商务报告加上一个适当的题目；在报告的正文中，也给不同的部分加入相应的标题。

考生在写作时还应当注意以下一些内容：

- 尽量使用丰富且恰当的词汇；
- 语法结构要避免单一；
- 根据写作任务要求确定语言的正式程度；
- 书写清晰、规范；

- 字数控制在 200 ~ 250 字。

2. 商务报告概述

商务报告是指针对某种特殊的、有意义的商务目的，向一个人或多个人提供的公正、客观和有计划的事实陈述。报告中所陈述的事实必须与事件、条件、质量、进展、结果、问题或提议的解决方案有关，帮助当事人了解复杂的商业情况，计划进程，解决问题，使决策者就一系列事件做出决策。

商务报告应用范围广泛，内容包罗万象，涉及了财务（finance）、审计（audit）、损益（profits & losses）、投资（investment）、年度（annual）、生产（production）、销售（sales）、市场分析（market analysis）、人事（personnel）等。

Day 5

商务报告的种类和四步写作法

1. 商务报告的种类

目前商务报告的分类方法多种多样，按报告的内容划分，常见的有：事件调查报告（Investigative Reports）；事故报告（Incident Reports）；意见调查报告（Survey Reports）；公差报告（Trip Reports）；定期报告（Periodic Reports），例如：周报告（Weekly Reports）、月度报告（Monthly Reports）；进展报告（Progress Reports）；市场调查报告（Market Research Reports）；审计报告（Audit Reports）；可行性研究报告（Feasibility Reports）等。

按照报告的格式划分，常见的有：便函体报告（memo report）、简短的文件体报告（short document report）和长篇商务报告（long formal report）。

此外，也可以根据商务报告的正式程度（level of formality）进行划分，可以划分为非正式报告（informal report）和正式报告（formal report）。

2. 商务报告的写作目的

一般情况下，商务报告有以下这些写作目的：

（1）提供信息；

（2）记录备查；

（3）提出建议；

（4）说服劝导。

3. 商务报告四步写作法

在撰写报告之前，应做好充分的准备。因此，撰写者应先回答以下几个问题：

- 报告的目的：为什么写这份报告？
- 报告的读者：谁是报告的读者？他（们）知道什么信息？他（们）需要什么信息？
- 报告的素材：撰写这份报告需要收集哪些信息？到哪里去收集这些信息？
- 报告的结构：如何构思报告？如何做到报告结构清晰，便于读者阅读？是否需要自己设计报告的格式还是公司有现成的格式可以参照？
- 报告的写作期限：报告何时须上交？

回答完以上问题后，可以按照以下四个步骤进行运作：

（1）收集信息（Collecting information）：收集信息可以采取口头或书面形式。口头形式包括面对面沟通或电话沟通获取信息等；书面形式指的是用办公室便函（memos）、电子邮件（emails）、问卷调查（questionnaires）等手段向公司内部或外部索取信息。此外，查阅公司的相关材料（如产品目录、价格单等）也属于书面收集信息形式。

（2）谋篇布局（Planning the structure）：确定报告写作的目的，对收集到的信息进行整理、分类，删除无关信息。然后按照信息的重要程度进行合理排列，列成提纲。若需要摆放插图或图表，也应在这一阶段确定其在报告中的位置。

（3）撰写草稿（Writing the draft）：撰写报告的各个部分。

（4）校对编辑（Proofreading and editing）：校对编辑报告写作的最后一个过程也是极其重要的一个过程，很遗憾这一过程往往被人忽视。撰写人写完草稿后应对报告进行全面检查，检查的具体内容包括两方面：一是语言，包括语法、拼写、标点符号、语言风格等；二是信息，包括数据、图表、观点等。检查后，应对报告进行编辑，尽量做到报告便于读者阅读。

Day 6

商务报告类题型语言表达特点

1. 商务报告总体写作原则

在撰写商务英语报告时，应确保报告内容准确无误（Accurate）、简明扼要（Brief），结构清晰（Clear），建议明确果断（Decisive），故简称“ABCD”原则。具体内容如下：

（1）内容准确无误（Accurate）：报告的正确性不仅仅是指英语语法、标点符号和拼写，更重要的是其内容要叙述的正确。报告的事实陈述部分既不能因哗众取宠而夸大其词，也不能因其涉及的令人不愉快的消息而低调陈述。实事求是、准确无误是报告写作的重要原则。

（2）内容简明扼要（Brief）：报告的长短一般取决于报告的内容及其正式程度。正式报告篇幅一般较长，而非正式报告则较短。不论何种报告，语言必须简洁、流畅，切忌陈词滥调。一份拖沓冗长的报告不仅写时费力，阅读更浪费时间。撰写商务英语报告时要尽量避免啰唆，用尽可能较少的文字，完整、清楚地表达需要表达的意思。

（3）结构清晰明了（Clear）：用数字、符号标明段落、层次、要点等，加强逻辑性，使读者一目了然。

（4）建议明确果断（Decisive）：多数报告都有结论和建议部分，是报告的核心。撰写时，应确保报告的结论和建议是经过充分论证而得出的，而且应明确果断，切忌模棱两可。

2. 商务报告的语言特征

➤ 条理

商务报告必须写得有条理，只有条理清楚，读者才能很快了解报告的写作目的、报告的主要内容以及报告的实际意义。一般情况下，分段是解决条理性这一问题最直接的办法。在商务报告写作中，考生可以根据所写的内容不同，将他们一一划归到不同的段落中去，然后再分别详细论述。此外，根据各个段落之间的关联，将他们划归到不同的部分中去，并且给每个部分加上相应的小标题，这样也能使商务报告条理清楚。

从结构上讲，在撰写商务报告时，首先应当注意一篇完整的商务报告大都包括以下几个方面：

- Overall title/Headings of each sections：报告的题目及每部分的标题
- Introduction：事由
- Findings：调查（比较）结果
- Conclusions：结论
- Recommendations：提出建议

➤ 逻辑

在商务报告的撰写中，还应当注意每一个部分之间的逻辑关联，如果第一部分是写事由（introduction），那么，在接下来的部分就应当展开具体的论述，证明并寻找调查结果（findings），最后得出结论（conclusions）并进行建议（recommendations）。如果我们在说明事由之后就直接提出建议，最后开展调查，这样看来，就会使文章显得混乱，有失逻辑。此外，在每个段落的论述中也应当关注语言的逻辑性。不能在提出一个论点之后就停止提供论据；在使用“because”时，“because”引导的从句必须要成为整个因果从句的原因。

➤ 衔接词（组）

观点之间的联系应当使用起衔接作用的词或者词组表达清楚，比如：“therefore，however，on the one hand，on the other hand…”等。同时也要会用引出下文的短语，比如：“There are a number of factors which…”等。

➤ 客观正式

商务报告的语言一般多为正式语体，主要是为了体现报告的客观性。一般来说，由于被动语态大都可以省略句子真正的主语，这样，就可以使文章显得正式、客观。比如："The findings are based on questionnaires…"，或者："Unless theses issues are investigated…"。除了被动语态，正式报告还常常使用很多的客观性语言，比如："It is important that …"（……很重要），"It would be better if …"（如果……会更好），"It is essential that action is taken immediately"。这类客观语言在文中提出建议，或者做出正式结论或者决策时，显得尤为重要，它可以使作者的观点客观有力，不带有明显的主观色彩。此外，广大考生也要积极运用正式词汇，口语中的常用词语尽量在撰写商务报告时替换为正式词语，例如："terminate" 就比 "end" 正式，"methods" 就比 "way" 正式。

以下就是一些经常出现在商务报告中的正式词汇：

selected

in terms of

in response to

further

legal compliance

employment practices

corporate philanthropy

participating organizations

ethical violations

legal violations

to indicate

level of management attention

of great concern

issue

respondents

➤ 简练

首先，在标题以及每个部分的小标题撰写时，名词或者名词短语就比句子简洁，在报告正文中，冗长的句子也往往可以用短小的词组或者短语来改写，比如："The staff feels deeply unhappy that management does not recognize their efforts". 这一句就可以改写成："A major staff complaint is lack of recognition".

其次，过去分词可以替代被动语态，例如："the issues which are identified" 就可以替换成："the issues identified"；并且动词的"ing"形式也可以代替从句，例如："the people who attended" 就可以替换成 "the people attending"。

最后，省略也可以实现行文简练的目的。省略就是指在意思一目了然的情况下，省掉一些词，例如："the next year sales decline down even more quickly than they did the year before." 在这一句子中，"they did" 就可以省略，这样可以避免重复，使句子短小精练。

下面请看具体的例子：

selected on the basis of size（分词，使句子简练）

an increasing level of interest expressed（分词，使句子简练）

when executives responding to our survey（分词，使句子简练）

written statements（分词，使句子简练）

participating organizations（分词，使句子简练）

an increase on the 22% reported（分词，使句子简练）

the two most frequently identified（分词，使句子简练）

...1, 000 Canadian companies, ~~which were~~ selected...（省略，使句子简练）

In response to an increasing level of interest ~~which was~~ expressed...（省略，使句子简练）

an increase on the 22% ~~which was~~ reported...（省略，使句子简练）

to indicate the level of management attention each ~~issue~~ received...（省略，使句子简练）

Of these issues, the two ~~issues which were~~ frequently identified...（省略，使句子简练）

3. 常见的商务报告表达形式

Introduction:

This report aims to...

This report sets out to...

The purpose of this report is to...

The report is based on...

Findings:

It was found that...

The following points summarize our key findings.

The key findings are outlined below.

Conclusion (s):

It was decided/agreed/felt that...

It is clear that...

No conclusions were reached regarding...

Recommendation (s):

It is suggested that...

It is proposed that...

It is recommended that...

We strongly recommend that...

It is essential to...

It would be advisable to...

Signaling:

The following areas of concern have been highlighted.

There are a number of reasons for...

There are several factors which affect...

A further factor is...

This raises a number of issues.

As might have been expected...

Contrary to expectations...

Day 7

商务报告类题型例文分析点评

1. 样题

Question 2

- Your company recently sponsored an event and the head of marketing has asked you to write a report about it.
- Write your report for the head of marketing:
  Outlining the reasons for choosing to sponsor the event;
  Describing the positive outcomes of sponsoring the event;
  Explaining the disadvantages that resulted from sponsoring the event;
  Making recommendations concerning future sponsorship activity.
- Write 200 – 250 words.

2. 例文初稿

Report on Sponsoring "2009 Super Girl"

Introduction

The purpose of this report is to find out the reasons of sponsoring "2009 Super Girl" which was held by Hu'nan TV and to evaluate the advantages and disadvantages of sponsoring this TV program so that the head of marketing could make reasonable decisions on whether they will go on doing it or not in the next year.

Findings

The reason for us to sponsor the "2009 Super Girl" is that our products aim at young customers. Statistics show that 80% of the juveniles are familiar with the program and they could sit in front of the TV from 8 p. m. till 10 p. m. every Saturday. The majority of our products are casual clothes for teenagers and juveniles, and most of them are fashionable enough to attract the potential TV viewers. Besides, all the candidates, hosts, and hostesses will put on our newly designed clothes, and they would make a public announcement during the break time that their closes are sponsored by our company. In this way, we will win a very good reputation.

After sponsoring the program, our sales rise up 50% than the sales of last year. Meanwhile, we have received more offers than what we did last year. However, due to sponsoring the program, our financial resources run low and we haven't enough equipment and labors to finish the tasks.

Recommendation

It would be advisable to make a detailed budget on the sponsoring activities in the following years. Besides, we should invest more on buying new equipment and hiring more skilled workers.

3. 例文点评

首先，该作文虽然字数符合要求，但是整体结构布局并不合理。虽然商务报告一般都包括“introduction, findings, conclusions 和 recommendation”，但是我们在实际写作时，可以根据写作内容的不同，调整每个部分的小标题。在写作要求中，考生应当注意到本文要求包括以下几个内容：原因、优缺点和建议。这样在报告中，我们就可以将标题改为：“introduction, reasons, advantages & disadvantages, recommendation”。修改后一目了然，给读者很清晰的印象，并且在写作时能够合理布局每一部分需要写的内容和所占的篇幅。这个范文初稿正是由于没有很好地把握这个结构布局，所以导致了在分析原因时占用了大量的篇幅，而第三段分析优缺点时却用很简单的三句话一带而过，没有充分地按要求完成写作任务。

其次，本习作语言不够简练。大家可以看到，在第一段“introduction”里只有一句话，但是却足足用了 58 个单词。冗长的句子里出现了很多的从句，烦琐的句式影响了清晰的表达。事实上，该句中的定语从句：“which was held by Hu’nan TV”完全可以换成分词或者介词短语的形式，比如：“on Hu’nan TV”；另外“whether they will go on doing it or not in the next year.”也可以直接换成名词短语：“future sponsorship”。

本习作中在“introduction”里分析原因时，没有逻辑关联的句子，影响了文章的清晰表达。比如：“they could sit in front of the TV from 8 p. m. till 10 pm every Saturday”这一句就和赞助的原因没有太直接的关联。过多地加入这样的句子且没有很好的衔接词来串联，就会有凑字数的嫌疑。

最后，本文中还有很多相同的信息重复出现，比如前边刚说：“our products aim at young customers”，后边又重复说“The majority of our products are casual clothes for teenagers and juveniles”。这样给人的感觉就很啰唆。

4. 例文修改稿

Report on Sponsoring “2009 Super Girl”

Introduction

This report aims to find out reasons of sponsoring “2009 Super Girl” on Hu’nan TV and evaluate this decision so as to guide next year’s sponsoring policy.

Reasons

The company sponsored this year’s “Super Girl”, as it would be shown on Hu’nan TV. It was hoped that this exposure would increase public awareness of the company name and its products because the candidates, hosts and hostesses will make recommendation to our casual clothes during the break time.

Advantages & Disadvantages

We commissioned a market research company to carry out an online survey in the week following the broadcast, and this showed a rise of five percentage points in public recognition of our name, compared with a year ago. In addition, sales jumped by nearly 50 percent immediately after the program, higher than at this time last year. Also, we have received more offers than last years since we sponsored it.

The cost of sponsorship was greater than expected, and had taken up over half the total marketing budget for the current financial year. The research found that too many offers brought another problem: it is impossible for the company to finish the tasks timely because we lack enough equipment and skilled workers.

Recommendation

It would be advisable that sponsorship should be based on the company's financial ability and strictly follow its annual budget. Besides, proper investment on new equipment and staff would contribute to the company's development.

Week 3

信函与建议书的写作攻略

Day 1

信函类题型特点

1. 写作任务解析

在第二题的写作中，一般都会要求考生根据要求写一篇字数在 200 ~ 250 字的一个商务信函，需要用 40 ~ 50 分钟来完成这部分的任务。这部分的题目要求有两点，一般第一点是给出一个写作环境，并且陈述要完成报告的一个具体背景；第二点中会列出在这个信函中应当写什么，写给谁，以及具体包括哪些内容（一般为 3 ~ 4 点）。考生需要设身处地地站在考试方要求的写作背景下，按照要求具体的完成这个写作任务。

考生在正式写作之前，最好是先勾勒一个写作提纲，并在提纲中简洁地标明每部分应当包括的内容。最好的办法是按照写作任务要求，逐一写出它规定应当包括的 3 ~ 4 点。在这里我们不建议大家调整这几点的顺序，因为一旦遗忘了一点，就会造成相应的失分。考生在写作时还应当注意以下一些内容：

- 尽量使用丰富且恰当的词汇；
- 语法结构要避免单一；
- 根据写作任务要求确定语言的正式程度；
- 书写清晰、规范；
- 字数控制在 200 ~ 250 字。

2. 商务信函的语言特点

写作商务信函并不要求使用华丽优美的词句。所有需要做的就是，用简单朴实的语言，准确的表达自己的意思，让对方可以非常清楚的了解作者想说什么。围绕这一点，我们总结了几方面的内容，希望对考生写作商务信函有借鉴作用。

➤ 正式程度

一般说来，商务信函较普通的私人信件来说都会更加正式一些。但是商务信函的正式与否由多方面因素决定。由于发信人与收信人的关系远近有别，职务有高低不等之差，他们所代表的实体也各不相同，加之商务信函的内容以及要解决的问题各不相同，这就造成了商务信函的正式程度也灵活多变。通常情况下，下级写给上级的信函就比较正式；如果以公司的口吻给合作伙伴写信，那么就相对正式；如果要给对方公司一个良好的印象，且表现出对对方公司足够的关注和重视，那么信函也大多很正式。相反，如果是公司内部同一级别的同事之间的信函，那就可以不用过于正式，不然会给对方拒千里之外的感觉；如果是一个非常熟悉的公司合作伙伴，那么，过于文书化的正式语言也会疏远两个公司之间的距离。因此，写商务信函时，首先要确定的就是这封信的正式程度。比如，在给潜在的客户寄来的抱怨信写回函时，就不太适合使用过于非正式的表达。因为较为正式的语言能够体现出公司对此事认真的态度和严肃处理决心，一封小小的信函也可以折射出员工的整体素质，公司的形象，并且对公司业务业绩产生深远的影响。

➤ 语气语调

由于商务信函都是有其目的性的，所以信函里所采用的语气语调也应该符合写作目的。在写之前先不妨仔细考虑一下，这封信函是想达到一个什么样的目的，希望对收信人产生一种怎样的影响，再根据实际情况，有的放矢的分别采用诸如直接、婉转、说明、劝说、道歉或强硬的语气传递信息，以达到写作目的。

➤ 真诚

不管是生活中的交往还是生意上的合作，真诚是最重要也是最基础的，所以您的信函也必须能够充分体现您的真诚。不管说什么，都要带着您的诚意去说。把写好的信函拿起来读一遍，确保如果此时对方正在电话中与您通话，他一定能够感受到您的自然和真诚。

➤ 直接

跟您一样，您的合作伙伴们每天都要阅读大量信函文件。所以，信函一定要写得简明扼要，短小精悍，切中要点。如果是不符合主题或者对信函的目的不能产生利益的内容，请毫不留情的舍弃它们。因为这些内容不仅不能使交流通畅，反而会混淆视听，非但不能让读者感兴趣，反而会让他们恼火，产生反感。

➤ 礼貌

商务信函，实际上是一种社交手段。我们这里所说的礼貌，并不是简单用一些礼貌用语比如“your kind inquiry，your esteemed order”等就可以的。而是要体现一种为他人考虑，多体谅对方心情和处境的态度。如果本着这样的态度去跟别人交流，那么就算您这次拒绝了对方的要求，也不会因此失去这个朋友，不会影响今后合作的机会。

特别要注意，当双方观点不能统一时，我们首先要理解并尊重对方的观点。如果对方的建议不合理或者对您的指责不公平时，请表现一下您的高姿态，您可以据理力争，说明您的观点，但注意要讲究礼节礼貌，避免用冒犯性的语言。这样做，不仅可以给对方留下很好的印象，还有助于建立良好的业务关系。即使我们拒绝了对方的要求，也不会影响双方在今后继续保持生意往来。

此外，礼貌也包含了体谅对方的态度。比如：应当第一时间处理对方需要答复的信函，一般情况下，商务信函应当在当天就回复，最晚不超过 24 小时，让对方过久的等候就是一种不礼貌的表现。如果不能迅速做出决策或者答复，那么至少也应当告知对方已收到来信，并且给出一个大致的时间。给对方的回复要迅速及时。因为依照常理，收信人通常只看最先收到的几封回复，从中去选择合适的供应商。如果您的回复不够及时，就可能因为抢不到先机而失去商机。

还要提醒一点，写商务信函时要注意一个原则：“过犹不及”。任何事情，一旦过了头，效果反而不好。礼貌过了头，可能会变成阿谀奉承，真诚过度，也会变成天真幼稚。所以最关键的还是要把握好“度”，才能达到预期的效果。

➤ 简洁

就像前面提到的，要用简洁朴实的语言来写信函，让您的信函读起来简单、清楚、容易理解。用常见的单词，避免生僻或者拼写复杂的单词。一个单词可以表达，就不要用词组。多用短句，因为短句更容易理解。少用“and”“but”“however”“consequently”这些让句子变得冗长的连词。在同一封信函里，不要使用多个相同含义的单词。比如，您前面写了“goods have been sent”，那后面再提到这件事时就不要再用其他单词如“forward”“dispatch”等。因为这样写会误导您的读者无谓地去考虑这些词之间是否另有含义。

➤ 精确

当涉及数据或者具体的信息时，比如时间、地点、价格、货号等，尽可能做到精确。这样会使交流的内容更加清楚，更有助于加快事务的进程。在提及收到的来信时，应该相应地提到它的日期、事由和主题，而不能笼统地说这封信是关于上月来信的回复。例如，我们应当准确地写出：“Thank you for your letter of 15th, February concerning...”。另外在说明时间时，尽量避免完全用数字写日期，比如：02/03/2009，因为这样的表达会让收信人对迷惑，不知道是3月2号还是2月3号。此外，在措辞上也要做到精确，即：拼写正确，词义正确，用法正确。比如说，尽量不使用有歧义或者多重含义的词汇，例如：“How do you account for the fact that the account is wrong?”最好是改成：“How do you explain the fact the account is wrong?”

➤ 针对性

请在邮件中写上对方公司的名称，或者在信头直接称呼收件人的名字。这样会让对方知道这封邮件是专门给他的，而不是那种群发的通函，从而表示对此的重视。当然，如果您无法确定收信人的名字，那就在称呼一栏里写“Dear Sirs”或“Dear Sir or Madam”。

➤ 语言结构丰富

语言结构丰富就是指，要避免行文单调贫乏。为了使行文丰富而富有变化，在写作过程中应该有意识地变换句式，尽量采用较丰富的句型结构。我们可以根据写作的需要，恰当地使用长短句、复合式的从句结构、正常语序和倒装语序、强调句、虚拟语气、疑问句等结构。比如说："I will call you as soon as I arrived"，如果全文过于单调，就可以改写成："As soon as I arrived，I will call you"。

➤ 标题

这一点是特别针对写电子邮件的。也许很多人都没有意识到，事实上，E－mail 的标题是很重要的一个部分，您的邮件给对方的第一个印象就是通过标题来完成的。如果标题没有内容，看起来像群发的垃圾邮件的话，很多买家就会直接删除。比如这样的标题"How are you?""Can we work together?"，建议您改成"Proposal：Bright Ideas Imports—Zhejiang Textile's Partnership Opportunity"或"Introduction：Our Product Offerings for Bright Ideas Imports."这样您的邮件会显得更加专业。

➤ 校对

写完之后，一定要检查。最基本是要确保拼写和语法正确，然后检查一下您所提供的事实，数据等是否有错。我们都会犯错，但即使在您的信函里有一个极小的失误，也可能会破坏您在沟通方面的可信度，并使人对您表达的其他信息投下怀疑的阴影。

Day 2

商务信函写作常用句型

Referring to previous contact

Thank you for your interest...

With reference to your letter of/dated...in which...

Further to our conversation of...

Starting the reason for writing

I am writing to confirm/apply for/outline...

I would like to thank/complain/comment on...

I am writing concerning...

As requested by the general manager, I am writing to outline...

Enclosing information

Please find enclosed...

As requested, I enclose...

Offering assistance

Should you have any further questions, please contact me on the above number.

If you require any further information, please do not hesitate to call me.

Referring to future contact

I hope to hear from you soon.

I look forward to hearing from you/meeting you/working with you.

Closing

Thank you for your attention/consideration...

If you have any further questions, please do not hesitate to contact me, either at the above address or on 123456.

Day 3

信函类题型例文分析点评

1. 样题

PART TWO

- You work for an employment agency. The following is part of a letter you have received from a customer:

The temporary administrative assistant you sent us was totally unacceptable. I certainly will not be using your agency again when I need temporary staff.

- Write a letter to the customer:
  - Apologizing for having sent the unsatisfactory temporary worker.
  - Giving reasons for what happened.
  - Explaining why what happened was exceptional.
  - Offering some sort of compensation to the customer.

2. 例文初稿

Dear Sir/Madam,

We are totally sorry about what happened in your company and we apologize for providing you with disqualified temporary administrative assistant. We will explain this issue thoroughly and hope our business cooperation will not be influenced by this accident.

I know that you are in need of an assistant urgently, so I was looking for a person who satisfied your need. The person I sent to your company give me an attractive résumé, on which he said that he was graduated from Cambridge University and he was good at computer programming, office administrating and team work. He also gave me two recommendation letters from former companies he worked before. Because we haven't enough time to call the companies he worked before, we didn't know that these recommendations were not real, and he actually didn't graduate from Cambridge University.

I am so sorry that this person caused you a lot of problem to your company. But this is an exception, because such things never happened in the past.

Because you suffered great losses in this period, we will make a sort of compensation to you. We will not charge for this case and will send you a new staff that has enough working experience in administration. I hope you could be satisfied.

Sincerely yours

3. 例文评语

该作文基本达到题目要求，字数也在规定的区间内。文章基本涵盖了要求写作的主要内容。但是行文不够简洁，且有些地方使用了超出考生自己实际能力的词汇，反而影响了表达和理解。另外该作文中的人称不一致，使读者觉得信件的口吻不太严肃和正式，道歉的态度不是很认真。

首先，在修改时，应当统一整个作文的人称。如果是以公司经理的口吻写这个道歉信，那么就统一用“I”；如果是用公司的名义写这个道歉信，那么就用“we”。最好不要在开头用“we”，中间没有任何铺垫的情况下又用“I”。

其次，句子要尽量简明，过长的句子容易引起混乱。考生应当检查自己所写的长句表达是否清晰。例如：“on which he said that he was graduated from Cambridge University”这一句中，就用了过多的词来搭建内嵌宾语从句的定语从句，但事实上这个句子的内在逻辑关系就比较混乱。

而且，考生应当学会去掉文章中不必要或者多余的表达。比如第一句中“We are totally sorry about what happened in your company and we apologize for”并列的两个主语都是“we”，且都代表同一主体，这样就可以把第二个“we”删掉。再比如，在第二段中，前一句已经说了“companies he worked before”，那下一句中就可以直接用代词来替换这个部分，而不是照抄。

再次，有些地方的表达不是很清楚，影响读者的理解。比如说：在第一段末尾应当用“incident”而不是“accident”；再比如说：“this person caused you a lot of problem to your company”，考生应当打好词汇基本功，明确应当是“cause + sb + adj”，或者是“cause sth to sb”，这一句正确的表达是“this person caused a lot of problem to your company”

最后，考生应当合理安排的字数和篇幅的布局。很明显，第三段在解释这是一个例外时，写作任务完成的并不是很充分，仅仅用了两个句子，阐述的不够透彻。

4. 例文修改稿

Dear Sir/Madam,

With reference to your letter of complaint about the assistant you received from my company, I would like to apologize. We deeply understand your losses and feel completely sorry about it, but we focus more on our customers and that is why we would like to give detailed reasons about what happened.

After a careful investigation, we have found out that the person you received was not as qualified as described in his resume. Shortly after you granted my company to provide a temporary assistant, we received this man's job application and arranged an interview. He told us that he was an administrative assistant and presented his resume, which said the person was graduated from University of Cambridge with an MBA degree. Besides, he said he had worked in many international companies and had accumulated sufficient experience. He also offered two recommendation letters from P&G, and the Royal Mail Service, which was turned out to be fake in the following investigation.

We would like to prove that this is an exception in the history of my company because it never happened before. Due to lack of experience and fully trust to the resume and recommendation letters, we ignored to check the signature and certificates enclosed. But we are sure that next time we will check all information either by phone call or by email so as to protect the interest of our customers and safeguard our reputation.

Giving the fact that this case caused you great loss, we would like to give you some compensation. We would send you a new assistant who was our administrative manager with 10 years' experience and his service is totally free of charge. We hope his performance will cater for your needs.

Yours faithfully

…

Day 4

建议书类题型特点

剑桥商务英语高级证书考试通常把商务建议书、简短商业计划、机构内部备忘录或简短商务报告，归于同一写作类型。考试写作的篇幅较短，一般限制在200～250个词汇之内。商务建议书或商业计划测试题可分成商务建议（计划）书和研究建议（计划）书两大类。考试时，考生撰写简短商务建议（计划）书要注意以下几点：

（1）建议（计划）书目标要明确且要合乎实际；

（2）实事求是地摆明实力或优势条件；

（3）具体明确地提出达到计划目标的办法和解决问题的措施；

（4）规定完成计划的时间。表明哪些做得到，哪些做不到，把握好分寸；

（5）确信解决问题的方法与实施项目的目标相一致。总之，商务建议（计划）书可以不拘一格，但是，建议（计划）书应当简洁清晰、立意完整、目标明确、论点鲜明、论据确凿、行文生动并有感染力和说服力。

简短商务建议试题主要分三大类：简短经营管理建议书、简短行政管理建议书和简短商业计划。文体框架和写法大同小异。

简短经营管理建议书的结构（Writing effective management proposal）

（1）交代建议书的主题和事由；

（2）针对主题提出论点；

（3）提出论据支持论点；

（4）提出建议。

简短行政管理建议书的结构（Writing effective administrative proposal）

（1）交代写建议书的起因和主题；

（2）指出存在的问题；

(3) 找出产生问题的原因;

(4) 提出解决问题的建议。

简短商业计划的结构 (Writing effective business plan)

(1) 简述商业计划背景;

(2) 列出事实依据;

(3) 根据事实进行推理分析,得出结论;

(4) 依据推理得出的结论提出商业计划,其中包括计划实现的目标以及达到目标的具体办法。

Day 5

建议书类题型语言表达要求

考生应试时，可以用简短商务报告或商业计划书的形式撰写商务建议，也可以用工作备忘录形式撰写简短商务建议，还可以用信函形式撰写商务建议。但是，无论选择何种文体，考生应遵循所选择的文体格式书写。考生必须仔细阅读考题要求，完全按照要求答题，既不要遗漏考题所要求的信息内容，也不要画蛇添足，随意添加考题没有要求的信息。

商务建议书写作提示：

Writing a business proposal is not an easy task, so here are some tips designed to help you write a winning proposal.

(1) Get as much information about the client as possible—annual reports, company periodicals, and publicity. Sometimes there is a point of contact, i. e. someone who is involved in drafting the request for proposals and who can answer technical questions about the form and content of your proposal. Call the person, they may reveal some information that can give you a competitive edge or at least a more customized approach to solving the prospective client's problem. Sometimes they even have a checklist of items they look for in each proposal and will be prepared to tell you about it if you ask.

(2) Prospective clients want to make sure you understand what they need before you start proposing a way to meet that need. If a reader needs to save money, you must slant all your ideas toward the goal of achieving cost effectiveness. If, for example, your department has a lot of experience in a specific area, then this fact should not just be mentioned but woven into a sentence highlighting how this experience could be of advantage to the client.

(3) Proposals are evaluated by a wide range of readers, from top management to technical evaluators to budget analyzers. These readers will focus on different sections of

a proposal, perhaps missing out whole segments. All readers, however, should be able to evaluate the first section of a proposal, which is a summary of the document. The length can vary greatly—it may sometimes be only one paragraph but in a very formal report it may run to several pages.

(4) The worst thing you can do is to offer value judgments that the client can refute. You want to seem serious, fair, objective and factual. Only after you build a foundation of fact can you offer a few judgments. Otherwise, you are likely to invite the reader to take issue with you. The facts are your findings and should be labeled as such: opinions are conclusions and should be labeled that way. If you use adjectives like "powerful" "wide-ranging" "significant", etc., make sure you support them with details.

(5) In proposal writing there is a tendency to rely on standard formats, i. e. static, standard sentences, paragraphs or pages that seem to fit all situations and do not change from proposal to proposal. No company sees itself as being like any other and so the last thing you want is for a prospective client to believe you are just recycling old solutions. You must try to create the ideas to fit the needs of the particular client and try not to copy old ideas because you cannot be bothered to generate new one.

Day 6

建议书类题型常见描述方法

1. 交代写建议书的起因

- As requested by the Managing Director, I have investigated the problems, which have been raised concerning office health and safety.
- The purpose of this report is to investigate the supervisors' training course in order to recommend new methods of training.
- The purpose of this report is to investigate staff use of company telephones for private calls so as to assess the scale of this practice.
- The purpose of this report is to investigate the relative costs of renting, buying and leasing photocopiers so as to establish the most efficient method.

2. 指出存在的问题

- In particular, I was asked to talk to office managers about any accidents or job-related illnesses, which may have occurred, and to make recommendations on how best to improve the situation.
- Absenteeism has reached its highest level for six years. Three years ago we had an average absentee level of 4% . Despite our proposals, laid down in the second five-year productivity plan, absenteeism has risen to around three hundred workdays lost per year.
- A distressing feature of absenteeism here is that only about a hundred of the workdays lost were officially reported, i. e. the absentee telephoned or sent a doctor's note. The other 65% gave no reasons for their absence. We recommend

that a new clause be added to the Contract of Employment.

3. 解释产生问题的原因

- A study was made of all accidents reported during the last twelve months. Three main causes were immediately clear.
- Imprecise terms of reference resulted in (or caused) an unsatisfactory report.
- Low demand resulted from (or was caused by) an expensive product.
- The high level of leasing resulted from (or was caused by) a higher level of taxation.
- Lack of interest in the Suggestion Scheme resulted from (or was caused by) low staff morale.
- The unsuitable photocopy service resulted from (or was caused by) poor maintenance of equipment.

4. 提出解决问题的建议

- A list of safety regulations should be clearly displayed in the company canteen and main offices.
- New staff should be informed of the company's safety regulations and policy.
- It should be the responsibility of the Personnel Manager to instruct all new staff on the procedures concerning the use of office equipment and machinery.
- All staff must exercise fire drill procedures at least twice a year.
- Office managers decided that old office equipment should be replaced with newer models particularly chairs without right back support.
- Employees who are absent without leave will have their earnings reduced by an amount equivalent to the number of hours lost.

5. 表示可能性

表示肯定、有把握（可能性达百分之百）

...will（definitely）reach

...are sure to reach

...are certain to reach...

表示很有可能（可能性超过 60%）

...will probably reach...

...should reach...

...are expected to reach...

表示有可能（可能性超过 30%）

...may reach...

...will possibly reach...

...could reach...

...might reach...

表示可能性不大（可能性低于 30%）

...probably won't reach...

...are unlikely to reach...

表示肯定达不到（没有可能性）

...will（definitely）not reach...

...are certain not to reach...

6. 结论/调查结果

In view of the high cost/the poor result/the success of indirect marketing/high turnover in sales staff/loss of existing clients/low return from foreign agents

7. 建议采取行动

强烈建议

- The follow-up sales calls must be made.
- National advertising must be stopped.
- It is strongly recommended that national advertising is (or be) stopped.
- National advertising should be stopped
- After-sales care must be improved.

中性建议

- It is recommended that telephone selling is (or be) stopped.
- It is advised to reduce telephone selling.
- It is advised to commission market research into agricultural equipment buyers.
- It is recommended to examine feasibility of using our own salesmen.
- It is advised to investigate competitors' salesmen's salaries.
- It is advised to reconsider rates of commission.

软性建议

- The appointment of a client relations manager could (or might) be considered.
- Rates of commission could (or might) be considered/raised.
- Salesmen's salaries could (or might) be considered/increased.

Day 7

建议书类题型例文分析点评

剑桥商务英语高级证书写作测试第二部分试题是撰写商务建议、简短报告或商务信函，考生可从中任选一题作答。请看以下有关商务建议的考题范例：

1. 样题 1

Your Managing Director has decided that the company's website should be improved and has asked you to consider ways of going about this.

Write a proposal for the Managing Director：

- Summarizing the strengths and weaknesses of the current website
- Suggesting new services and information to be provided through the website
- Explaining the benefits the improvements would bring

Write 200 – 500 words on the separate answer paper provided.

2. 样题 1 例文及点评

To：Mr. Clark，Managing Director

From：John Walker，Head of the Administrative Department

Date：Feb. 28，2006

Proposal on Improving Company's Website Service

The aim of this report is to summarize the strengths and weaknesses of the current website，and recommend new services and information to be provided through the website.

Strengths

Our website can streamline business processes to improve operating efficiencies. Based on information provided by current website, we can analyze past customer behavior to anticipate customers' needs, thus allowing suppliers and customers controlled access to the date they need.

We now have greater ability to offer goods and services to the consumer over the Web. We can present goods more effectively, take orders and invoice on-line. This means improving margins for the business and a faster, more responsive service for customers. We have built, through website, our reputation on personal service and high quality products.

Weaknesses

We have to take on more expenses, because we need to provide 24 – hour website service/back-up. We also need to keep up-to-date with technical advances to tackle the potential systems failures (viruses).

The customers need to have reliable Internet access. At present, many e-commerce customers lack of confidence in system security. It's hard for consumers to trust e-commerce when they can't see the practices behind the promises.

Recommendation

I wish to recommend a portfolio of on-line service, merging online files with data collected about individuals' off-line purchase to better target promotions, thus remarking our website into a popular Web departing from its once-serious image. With new offerings, the content makeover should lure enough users into portal and keep them there long enough for the company to raise advertising and e-commerce sales to larger revenue.

点评：

建议书标题“改进公司网站服务的建议”，直接点出建议书主题。全文分四个部分。第一部分：开门见山，直接提出写建议书的目的。第二部分：列举公司网站的优点。第三部分：列举公司网站的弱点或不足。第四部分：提出改进公司网站的建议。这是以简短报告的形式撰写的简短商务建议书。包含了试题所要求的几点内容，语言简洁、流畅、规范，可供模拟。

3. 样题 2

You are the head of the Administrative Department of a company. The Managing Director has asked you to write a proposal for office health and safety provisions.

Write a proposal for the Managing Director:

- Giving reasons for writing the proposed proposal
- Summarizing the problems that have been raised concerning office health and safety
- Giving the main causes of the possible accidents
- Suggesting new provisions of office health and safety

Write 200 – 250 words on the separate answer paper provided.

4. 样题 2 例文及点评

To: Mr. Gates, Managing Director

From: John Smith, Head of the Administrative Department

Date: March 18, 2006

Subject: Office Health and Safety Provisions

As requested by the Managing Director, I have investigated the problems, which have been raised concerning office health and safety. In particular, I was asked to talk to office managers about any accidents or job-related illnesses, which may have occurred, and to make recommendations on how best to improve the situation.

A study was made of all accidents reported during the last twelve months. Three main causes were immediately clear:

— faulty equipment;

— failure to follow safety regulations;

— insufficient knowledge on the part of new staff about health and safety procedures.

I also studied records of all job-related illnesses during the past year. Meetings were held to discuss what could be done.

Proposals:

— A list of safety regulations should be clearly displayed in the company canteen and main offices.

— New staff should be informed of the company's safety regulations and policy.

— It should be the responsibility of the Personnel Manager to instruct all new staff on the procedures concerning the use of office equipment and machinery.

— All staff must exercise fire drill procedures at least twice a year.

— Office managers decided that old office equipment should be replaced with newer models, particularly chairs without right back support.

点评:

建议书标题“办公室卫生和安全措施”。全文分三部分。第一部分交代写建议书的原因和目的。第二部分简述调研结果，找出过去一年中发生安全事故及疾病的原因。第三部分提出改进办公室安全和卫生状况的措施。全文语言简洁流畅，层次分明，可供模拟。

Week 4

解析试题与写作练习

Day 1

试题解析与练习（Test 1）

Test 1

WRITING 1 hour 10 minutes

PART ONE

➤ Question 1

- The graphs below show the performance of a European country's manufacturing and agricultural sectors in terms of exports and imports between 1991 and 2001.
- Using the information from the graphs, write a short report describing the general movements in exports, imports and the resulting balance of trade.
- Write **120 – 140** words.

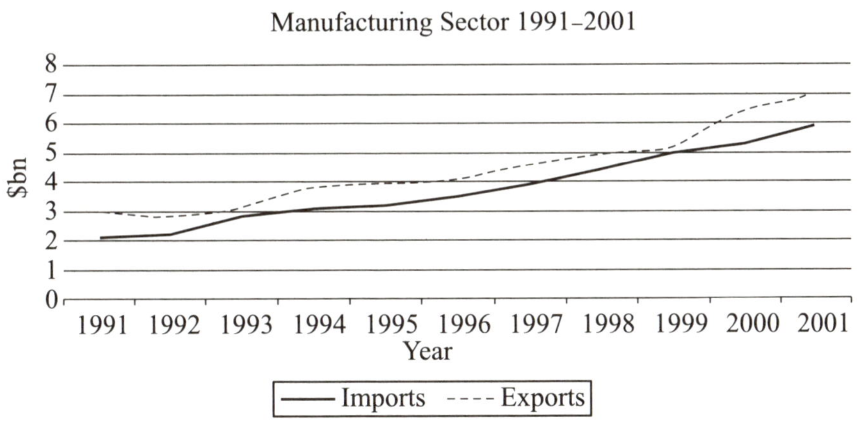

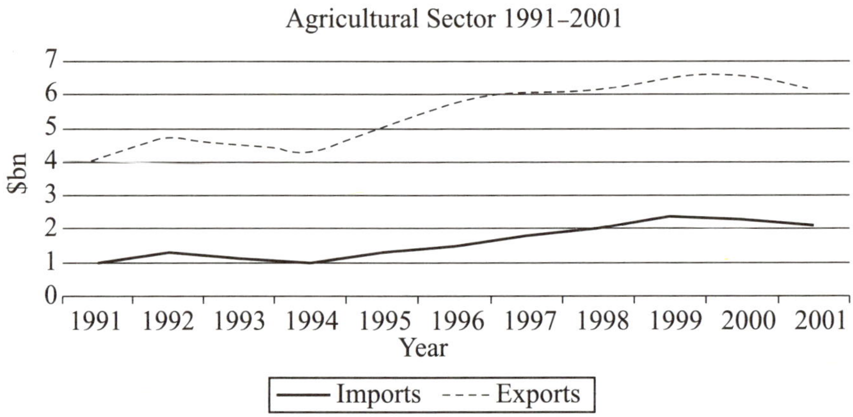

PART TWO

Write an answer to **ONE** of the questions 2 – 4 in this part. Write your answer in **200 – 250** words.

➤ Question 2

- The Managing Director of your company or organization has announced that reports on performance are to be produced by all departments. Your Head of Department has asked you to produce the report about your department for the Managing Director.
- Write the **report** for the Managing Director, explaining:
  - · What aspects of your department function most effectively
  - · Which aspect is most in need of improvement
  - · How this improvement could be achieved.

➤ Question 3

- You work for an employment agency. The following is part of a letter you have received from a customer:

The temporary administrative assistant you sent us was totally unacceptable. I certainly will not be using your agency again when I need temporary staff.

- Write a letter to the customer:

- Apologizing for having sent the unsatisfactory temporary worker
- Giving reasons for what happened
- Explaining why what happened was exceptional
- Offering some sort of compensation to the customer.

➤ Question 4

- Your Managing Director has decided that the company's website should be improved and has asked you to consider ways of going about this.
- Write a **proposal** for the Managing Director:
  - Summarising the strengths and weaknesses of the current website
  - Suggesting new services and information to be provided through the website
  - Explaining the benefits and the improvements would bring.

Sample answers to Test 1

➤ Question 1

Sample A

This report describes the movements of the balance of trade between 1991 and 2001, for a particular country, concerning manufacturing and agriculture.

Manufacturing

Imports increased constantly during this period. The figure shows a rise of \$4bn within the whole period and no fluctuations are to be remarked.

Exports rose from nearly \$3bn in 1991 to approximately \$7bn in 2001, suffering minor fluctuations all the way through. In general, the balance of trade remained slightly positive through the period considered.

Agriculture

Imports increased slightly, ending the period around \$1bn over their starting level. They suffered a temporary fall between 1992 and 1994, followed by a steady recovery. After peaking at around ＄2.5bn in 1999, imports fell slightly to their final value.

Exports figure shows the same performance although at level ＄4bn higher than imports.

Consequently, the balance of trade remained markedly positive throughout the period.

Band 4

点评：该篇较好地完成了写作任务，并且能够涵盖题目要求的全部内容。作者对于语言的使用比较自然，能够较为娴熟地运用动词的现在分词及过去分词做状语。但仍然有少量的语法错误，比如在介词的使用上，单复数一致以及表达准确性等问题上。作者全文布局合理，对于连接词的运用，如“in general, consequently”较好地体现了严谨的文章结构和谋篇布局。文章词汇量较为丰富且用法准确，在表达“大概”这个意思时使用了“nearly”“approximately”及“around”等不同词汇，但某些词的使用稍欠妥当，比如在介词短语“between...and...”的使用上。

➤ Question 2

Sample B

This report aims at outlining which aspects of our department function most effectively, which ones need improvement and how to achieve an efficient improvement.

First of all, it needs to be stressed out that the majority of the team generally shows a real team spirit, is willing to do his best to prioritize some smooth interactions with customers and is not reluctant to work outside the normal working hours.

On top of that, every member of the team has been carefully selected for his/her excellent qualifications in terms of negotiating skills and communications abilities.

As a result, it came out of the recent survey, conducted with most of our customers, that our department has an excellent image outside the company.

Unfortunately, however, some aspects appear to be less brilliant. As part of our sales force, people spend most of their time on the phone and cannot fit any training course within their schedule. As there is no clear strategy to encourage the employees to attend training courses, they may feel guilty to decide to use part of their working time to get a better knowledge on a computer software for instance.

This being, said, I strongly recommend to define a clear strategy encouraging people to register, at least, to two training courses, each year.

This would help them to understand that, whatever their initial qualifications may be, it may bring benefit to both them and the company to improve them.

Band 3

点评：该习作基本完成了写作任务，题目所要求的主要内容大致包括在内，但一些重要内容仍未能详尽陈述。作者对于词汇的运用基本准确，对于衔接词如"first of all, on top of that, as a result, unfortunately"的使用上较为熟练。全文布局合理但稍显松散，如第二、第三自然段就可以合并成一个自然段，最后两个自然段也是如此。本文语言基本准确，有少量的语法错误，如一个句子中出现了两个动词而之间没有连接词的情况。有些句式使用较为口语化，如"this being, said..."但这并不影响读者对于全篇文章内容的理解。

➤ Question 3

Sample C

Dear Sir,

In response to your letter of complaint about the employer you received from my company, I would like to apologize. We know and understand your complaints but we really care about our customers and that is why in this letter we will try to give our reasons about what happened.

The person you received last week was a lier. One week before you asked for the employer, this young man came into my office and told me he was an administrative assistant and showed me his CV. In the curriculum he presented to me, he was wonderful, it said that this person was graduated from Oxford University with a wonderful average, and his work experience was very extended. Two weeks ago I heard from a friend that this young man bought his CV and did not have it.

This is the first time in the history of my company that this happens. I would like to tell you that this case was exceptional. This young man came to my office for certain circumstances but I am sure this will not happen again. But to be sure the next time I get a CV I will call to all numbers written on it, to be certain that the employer is not a lier.

Knowing that this case is exceptional and giving you the reason of your complaint, I would like to give you some kind of compensation. Next week, if you like, I will send you another administrative assistant, free of company's charge. I hope you reconsider this chance and write back an answer.

Yours faithfully

…

Band 3

点评：本文较为合理地完成了写作任务，基本涵盖了题目要求的主要内容。文章结构合理，语言使用基本准确，但仍有一些词汇和语法错误，比如“骗子”的英文说法并不是“lier”，而应该是“liar”。在倒数第二个自然段中，作者对于动词现在分词的用法也稍欠妥当。在对于句式的把握上，作者完成得比较好，但有些句式，如“but to be sure the next time I…”并不是准确的英文表达方式。虽然有些词语的使用并不妥当，但全文的语气基本符合书信的表达习惯，整篇文章尚能被读者所接受。

➤ Question 4

Sample D

PROPOSAL ON WAYS TO IMPROVE XYZ'S WEBSITE
NOVEMBER 2002

This proposal aims to set out various ways and possibilities available in order to improve our website.

SWOT Analysis

As a result of a SWOT analysis, the following points summarise our main findings.

- Strengths

We were the first major company in one sector to set up a website.

We benefit from a very high rate of brand recognition and therefore internet users remember or find our site easily through search engines.

- Weaknesses

Out of date: Despite being the innovators when launching our website, the information provided online is, in many cases, out of date (prices, phone numbers).

Not user friendly. The structure of our paper is very rigid, potential customers cannot, do not have freedom of movement.

No online purchase facility available.

Suggestions and Recommendations

It was felt that in order to remain ahead of our competitors we should carry out some of the following improvements.

- A more user friendly website allowing the user to have more freedom. Then, surveys have shown that such facility increases sales.
- Regular update of the information and services available.

  Such update will encourage our clients to consult our paper regularly and to keep them inform on any specific sale.

- Online purchase facility.

  It was felt that his facility is now a must-have for every big company.

  Such facility will also enable us to collect precious data which imported into our database will be a good marketing tool.

  By doing so we should be able to keep our clients informed when we have sales on their favourite purchase.
- Online Newsletter Again, the use of our database could improve significantly our customer communication—such newsletter could be produced on a quaterly basis.
- FAQ a Frequent Ask Questions should be instaured.

Benefits of such improvements

Most benefits have been explained above, however, we recommend strongly to carry out such improvements as soon as possible.

This might be possible either by training our in-house marketing team on website production and management or by contracting a web designer specialist. We would like to highlight the fact that although e-mail marketing is a very powerful tool, we must keep up to date with any legislation regarding data protection.

Band 4

点评：该习作完成得比较好。文章涵盖了题目要求的所有内容，阐述较为清晰。作者语言的使用比较自然，能够娴熟地使用长短句式，对于比较复杂的句式，如“either...by...”都能够准确使用。本文运用了丰富的词汇且使用比较准确。但文章中也存在着少量的语法错误，如主谓一致问题。某些句子的表达不准确，如“potential customers cannot, do not have...”中，“cannot”与“do not”只保留一个即可。作者布局比较合理，每一个要点都用 ABC 表达得非常清晰，但文章有些标点符号的使用不够准确。

Day 2

试题解析与练习（Test 2）

Test 2

WRITING 1 hour 10 minutes

PART ONE

➤ **Question 1**

- The bar charts below show levels of wheat production and wheat prices in a European country for the period 1990 – 2000.
- Using the information from the bar charts, write a short **report** summarizing the changes in production and prices between 1990 and 2000.
- Write **120 – 140** words.

WHEAT PRODUCTION AND PRICES

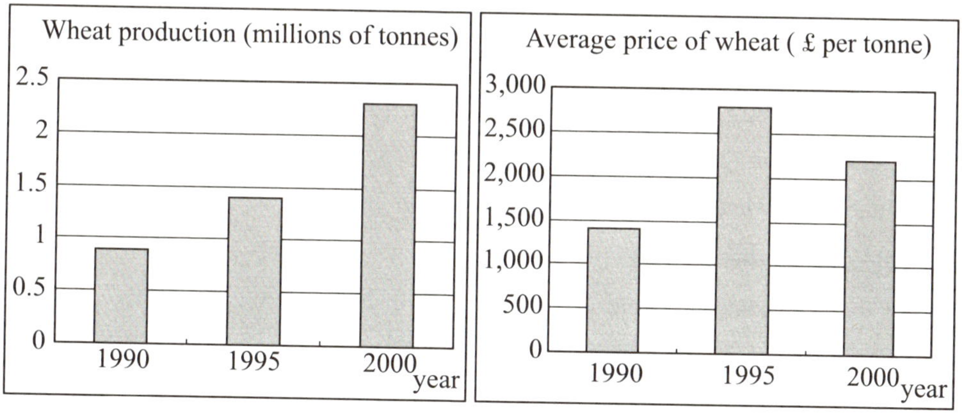

PART TWO

Write an answer to **ONE** of the questions 2 – 4 in this part. Write your answer in **200 – 250** words.

➤ Question 2

- You have recently attended the following one-day courses:
  - Developing Your Potential;
  - Trends in Electronic Commerce;
  - Managing People;
  - Reducing Costs.

  Your company's Training Manager has asked you to write a short report about the training.
- Write the **report** for the Training Manager:
  - Describing the two courses which you found most useful;
  - Explaining how you benefited from them;
  - Outlining the specific training courses you would like to attend next year;
  - Giving reasons why these courses would be useful to you.

➤ Question 3

- Your manager has asked you to contact a local business school, inviting their students to apply for a three-month work placement in your company.
- Write a letter to the Principal of the business school:
  - Introducing your company and the idea of the placement;
  - Describing what work the placement would involve;
  - Explaining what skills and qualities the successful applicant should have;
  - Saying how the placement would benefit the applicant.

➤ Question 4

- The Sales Director of your company wants to improve customer service and believes that this can be achieved by extending the opening hours of the Sales Department. He has asked you to write a proposal concerning improvements in customer service.

- Write a proposal for the Sales Director:
  - · Summarising current problems concerning customer service;
  - · Evaluating the Sales Director's suggestion;
  - · Presenting one or two other measures which could be taken;
  - · Giving reasons for your preferred course of action.

Sample answers to Test 2

➤ Question 1

Sample A

Introduction

The aim of this report is to summarise the changes in production and average prices of wheat between 1990 and 2000.

Findings

Focusing our attention on wheat production, it can be seen from the graph that the output rose steadily over the period. A general upward trend from 0. 9 millions of tonnes in 1990 to 2. 3 millions of tonnes in 2000 is clearly recognizable.

On the other hand, the average price of wheat totaled 1, 400 £/T in 1990, but in 1995 it increased rapidly reaching a peak of 2, 900 £/T. In 2000 the price fell to 2, 400 £/T which was however more than the minimum price in 1990.

Conclusion

As can be seen from both graphs average price of wheat did not show the same characteristics as total wheat production.

Band 4

点评：该习作较好地完成了题目要求的写作任务，结构比较清晰，所用词汇和短语较丰富，例如："focus on，reach a peak"；能运用恰当的连接词如"on the other hand"，并且能够用到"focusing on"这样的分词放在句首做状语的结构。句型的使用也较丰富，如："it can be seen that…，as can be seen from…"，等等。但也有小的错误，例如："more than the minimum price"．结尾部分表达欠佳，但并不影响整篇文章给人的好印象。

➤ Question 2

Sample B

Report：Training Courses

Introduction

The aim of this report is to summarise and assess the training courses I have recently attended for the use of the Training Manager.

Courses

In my opinion，the most useful courses were：

- Managing People
- Trends in Electronic Commerce.

"Managing People" was a one-day course focused on management techniques and their successful implementation. It examined different management styles and their benefits and disadvantages.

"Trends in Electronic Commerce" was a practically oriented one-day course. The main issues discussed involved：the latest trends in e-commerce，security of information，business to business（B2B）trading and potential savings enabled by e-commerce.

Benefits

Both of these courses were very interesting for me，as I work as a Purchase Manager. I am going to use some of the management techniques in my department. I would like to improve the current approach to motivation or organization of meetings for example. I think that "motivating people" is a key aspect of my job. "Trends in Electronic Commerce" course was also very useful for me as we are set to start ordering process using the Internet technology.

Conclusion

Next year, I would like to attend at least one of the following courses:

- Effective Negotiations,
- Time Management,
- Communication—a key factor for success.

As all of these topics are closely related to my profession, I am sure that it would be to my and also company's benefit if I could attend these courses.

Band 4

点评：这是一篇比较好的习作，能够完成题目要求的所有写作任务。文章结构清晰，让人一目了然。语言使用清楚得当，词汇运用比较丰富。能够使用"I would like to"等表达句式，并能正确运用定语从句，例如："the training courses I have recently attended for the use of the Training Manager". 连接词的运用也较恰当如"as"。但文章中也有小的错误，例如："would be to my and also company's benefit"，此外时态的运用稍显混乱。

➤ Question 3

Sample C

27 March 2003

To: Mr. Thomas George

Invitation for a three-month placement for students in Zee Online Education Ltd.

Dear Sir,

Zee Online Education is a leading multinational company in the field of online learning

& e-learning. We offer specialized online courses in Computer Software. These courses are recognized by the government and also internationally. We would like to offer placements for a short period to students from your business school.

The placement job would require students to do market research on certain important issues. Some of the areas of market research would be a) New Software required for the latest trends in the IT market. b) How well are online courses encouraging the growth of employment. c) Geographical area—relating to added use of a particular software. E. g: Places in the South of India like Coimbatore find that courses for textile design or CAD (Computer Aided Design) are popular—this is due to the large number of textile mills in the area.

Market research involves a lot of confidence on the part of Students. An eye for detail, a pleasing personality and an assertive attitude would be a plus factor for a Student working in the area of market research. Connecting with people would be another factor. Students must be able to mingle freely with employees of the company they are researching with. People skills help students go a long way in the areas of market research.

A job placement like this would definitely be an added advantage to a student's résumé. It would give him a wealth of experience in a short span of time. Fresh with the knowledge gained from the course a student will be able to gain hands on experience, which will benefit the next step that he takes in his career.

Yours Sincerely

…

Band 4

点评：该文是一篇比较好的习作，完成了题目中要求的所有写作任务。尽管开头和结尾处所用的信函格式不正确，但整体的语言使用自然，一些短语和习惯用法的运用得当，例如："an eye for detail, in a short span of time, fresh with the knowledge"。信函中使用了非常得体的礼貌表达方式，例如："we would like to, the placement job would require students to do… "。词汇的使用也比较丰富，并且能够正确运用一些词语结构和句型，例如："require sb. to do…, relate to…, due to…"，定语从句 "employees of the company they are researching with"。但也存在语法错误，如："people skills help students go a long way"。

➤ Question 4

Sample D

As it has been decided that changes in the customer service of the company ought to be made, the following points are brought up for attention:

1. Existing customer service is inadequate because:

   a) It is too slow in the attention to the client, and

   b) very often erroneous information is given to the client.

Summarizing: There is an evident waste of time and loss of client variability.

2. Extending opening hours of the Sales Department, as suggested by the Sales Director will solve the problem only partially due to the fact that—

   a) Not sufficient clients need the service during after-hours, and

   b) the root of the problem springs from the initial delay the customer generally has to suffer.

3. Additional measures that should be studied for possible approval are:

   a) Passing phone enquiries directly to a call centre.

   b) Training junior salesman in customer service policy of the company.

4. The selection of the above listed measures is based on the following information

gathered from the Marketing and Personnel Departments as well as from a considerable amount of data obtained directly from the client and which pinpoint the following flaws:

a) Clients who telephone the company complain regularly of the excessive time they are kept hanging on the line until someone attends them.

b) Another regular complaint from clients is that junior salesman are often unfamiliar or doubtful as to the after sales guaranty and services to which they are entitled when they have purchased one of our products.

It seems obvious that junior salesmen are not getting sufficient training and that a possible special training programme for them would solve the problem in a short time and with little additional expenditure.

Band 4

点评：这篇习作较好地完成了题目中所要求的任务。文章连贯，结构清晰。语言使用比较自然。能够正确运用一些比较复杂的句型，例如："as it has been decided that..., clients who telephone the company..., it seems obvious that..."。词汇和短语的使用比较丰富，例如："sufficient, pinpoint, considerable, as well as, is based on..."。尽管存在几个小的语法错误，但并不影响其成为一篇较好的文章。

Day 3

试题解析与练习（Test 3）

Test 3

WRITING 1 hour 10 minutes

PART ONE

➤ Question 1

- The chart below shows the percentages of a company's turnover which were contributed by its main product areas in three successive years.
- Using the information in the chart, write a short report comparing the contributions of the three products to turnover in the three years.
- Write **120 – 140** words on a separate sheet.

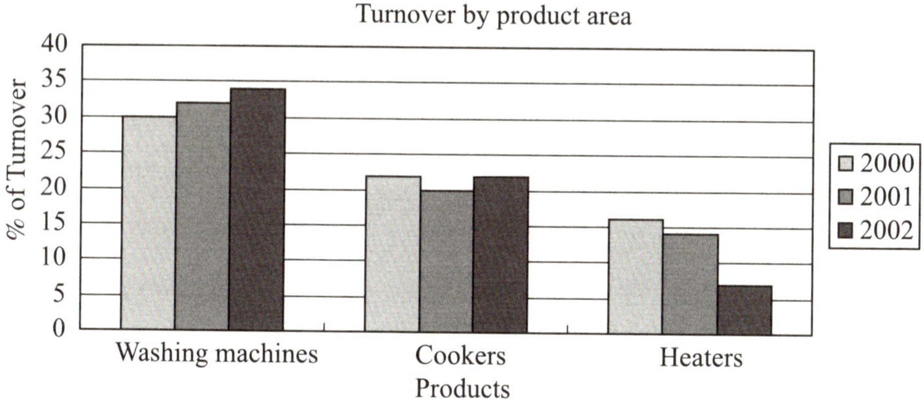

PART TWO

Write an answer to ONE of the questions 2 – 4 in this part. Write your answer in **200 – 250** words on a separate sheet.

➤ Question 2

- The Sales Manager in your company is looking for a venue where he can hold a three-day conference for sales staff. You have recently attended a conference at the Marston Conference Centre and the Sales Manager has asked you to prepare a report on the suitability of the Centre for his conference.
- Write your report for the Sales Manager:
  - Describing your experience of the venue when you attended the conference there;
  - Assessing the positive and negative aspects of the venue;
  - Making a recommendation as to its suitability for your company's conference.

➤ Question 3

- You are dissatisfied with the poor service that has recently been provided by the company responsible for delivering your products to your customers.
- Write a letter to the company:
  - Informing them of the fall in the standard of their service;
  - Explaining why you are dissatisfied;
  - Describing the bad effect the service has had on your business;
  - Detailing what action you intend to take if the service does not improve.

➤ Question 4

- You feel that your company's main product or service would benefit from better publicity. The directors have asked you to write a proposal putting forward your ideas.
- Write your proposal for the directors:
  - Mentioning the product or service concerned;
  - Stating the shortcomings of the current advertising;
  - Outlining how your competitors publicise their products or services;
  - Suggesting a different approach to advertising.

Sample answers to Test 3

➤ Question 1

Sample A

The chart shows how much of the turnover of a certain company was contributed by each of its three main product areas in the years 2000, 2001 and 2002.

Generally speaking, washing machines are the strongest and heater the weakest of the three products. This basic difference between the two became even more pronounced in this three years period with the contribution of washing machines to the company's turnover rising from thirty percent in 2000 to thirty-four percent in 2002, while the share which the heaters contributed dropped from sixteen percent in 2000 to seven percent in 2002. The contribution of the third product—cookers—remained relatively steady during this period; it dropped slightly from twenty-two to twenty percent in 2001, but recovered again in 2002.

Band 5

点评：这是一篇非常优秀的习作，出色地完成了题目要求的写作任务。全文表达清晰、语意连贯，涵盖了图表中的主要内容。作者规划了段落，布局合理，结构清晰，明确表达了要表述的内容。第二段段首所用“Generally speaking”，是写作中常用的连接语，可以极好引出下文。文中复杂句的使用也很出彩，条理清楚，运用得当。再从语言上看，作者使用词汇较丰富，如“basic，contribution，steady”等，清晰且恰当地描述了图表。整体来说，虽文章末尾并未总结，且至最后一句才提到厨具，但并不影响其通篇效果，它给人的印象仍然是一部佳作。

➤ Question 2

Sample B

This report aims to describe the Marston Conference Centre and to make a recommendation as to its suitability for the upcoming three-day conference for sales staff. The information and recommendation are based on the experience I had as a participant at the marketing conference held there two weeks ago. Here is a brief outline of the points I believe ought to be considered:

Location: the conference center is not far from the highway and also easy to reach by public transport (trains to the village run every hour) and the center's shuttle service.

Accommodation: A hotel next to the center offers approximately 170 well-equipped single rooms. There are, however, no other hotels in the immediate neighborhood of the center.

Conference Rooms: the center features twelve rooms of various sizes (10 – 1, 200 persons), all of them equipped to the latest standards of conference technology. Only three of them are equipped with a mobile stage, however.

Food: A restaurant and a bar at the conference center cater to the participants' needs, serving delicious food at reasonable prices. The restaurant is open from 11: 00 a. m. until 11: 00 p. m., the bar usually closes at about 2: 00 a. m. Service is well-organized and speedy.

Staff at the center: staff at the center is very well-trained, highly professional, helpful and friendly and available 24 hours a day.

Surroundings: the center is surrounded by a large park with ponds, benches and the like an ideal place for socializing in breaks.

I would highly recommend holding the conference at the Marston Conference Center as it is.

Band 4

点评：该文作者比较出色地完成了写作任务，语言使用比较自然，词汇运用丰富。通篇表意连贯，正式得体，写作格式比较恰当。只是最后表述并未完成，没达到预期的表达效果。不过整体而言，此文几乎涵盖了题目要求的所有内容，结构清晰，语言得当，是一篇较为优秀的习作。

➤ Question 3

Sample C

Maria da Silva
Boticario Brasil
32, Park Avenue
Sao: Paulo SP

Mary Higgins
Customer Service
Wzd Transport
9, Wind Road
Sao Paulo SP

May 17, 2003

Dear Mr. Higgins,

Boticario brasil has had a contract with your company for the last four years, since we decided to outsource our delivery service. The main reason for us to do so was because at the time we felt that a reliable business partner could better our distribution and reduce costs.

Your deliveries were satisfactory until last Christmas; however, since January we have been finding the standard of your service absolutely below expectations. Last April, when we were in the midst of launching our new product line, your company failed to deliver our loads to 3 of our major retailers, 2 of them being very important high street sites. Needless to say this had a terribly negative effect on our sales. We had just invested in a high-impact advertising campaign, and when our consumers went to the shops, the products simply were not there on the shelf.

In April we were faced with yet another problem due to your poor service, when a delivery to Rio de Janeiro was 20 days late.

I do hope you address this matter as top priority and re-establish the good service you used to provide, or else, Boticario will have to look for another business partner.

I look forward to hearing from you.

Yours Sincerely

Band 4

点评：这是一篇比较优秀的习作，较为出色地完成了写作任务，题目要求所有内容均已涵盖。从语气和口吻来看，这封商务信函符合题目所设置的背景要求，用词得当，表达清晰。作者对于商务信函的写作格式比较熟悉，运用恰当。全文布局合理，各段落依照写作目的一一展开，准确地表达了要表述的内容。此外，正文中使用了“Needless to say; I do hope; or else”等表达，起到了加强语气的作用，强调了表述目的。总的来说，该信函表意明确，语言得体，给人印象较为深刻。

➤ Question 4

Sample D

Proposal for a new marketing campaign

Introduction

The purpose of this proposal is to recommend some changes in our advertising campaign concerning our mobile phones for business use. Our market share in this sector has slightly fallen, despite of our technological leadership in constructing such devices.

Findings

We are advertising our high end model in the same medias like our other products.

However, our target group are business executives. Therefore it would be advisable to place our advertisements in the Financial Times. We should also think about advertising in some business journals.

We should change some aspects of our advertisements. It would be a good idea to have pictures with people in business related situations, for example in meetings or in the business lounge at the airport. We should also focus on some key facts which are important for business executives. We should mention that we implemented every standard of mobile communication and that our phones can be used everywhere in the world.

Our competitors always state the weight of their phones and the quality of their energy units. We should make clear that our phones are superior even concerning these aspects. And of course our design is more sophisticated.

Conclusion

To sum up, we should make some changes where we advertise and also the content of our advertisements.

Recommendations

We strongly recommend to implement the above measurements in due course.

Band 3

点评：该习作基本完成了写作任务，满足了题目的主要要求。词汇使用丰富，表述较为清晰。通篇划分段落，布局比较合理。只是总结部分过于简单模糊，表意不明确。文章末尾所提建议，有些多余，显得累赘。文章语言使用不太自然，但极少出现语法错误，且并未出现妨碍理解的表述。

Day 4

试题解析与练习（Test 4）

Test 4

WRITING　1 hour 10 minutes

PART ONE

➤ Question 1

- An international survey has recently been conducted, asking whether companies plan to alter their spending on information technology next year. The pie charts below compare planned expenditure on IT by European and South – East Asian companies in the coming year.
- Using the information from the pie chart, write a short **report** describing the differences between Europe and South – East Asia.
- Write **120 – 140** words.

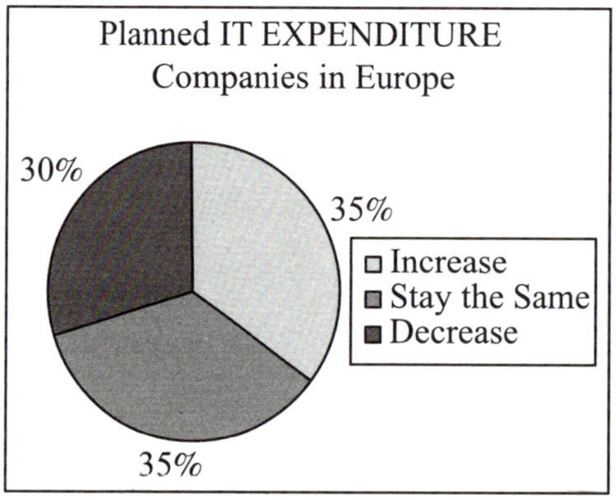

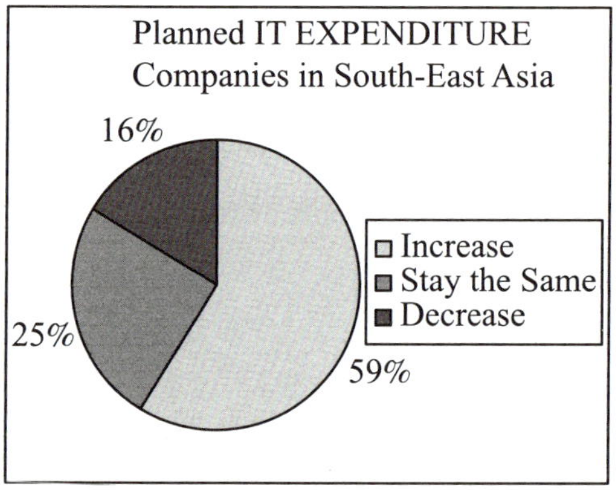

PART TWO

Write an answer to **ONE** of the questions 2 – 4 in this part. Write your answer in **200 – 250** words on a separate sheet.

➤ Question 2

- Your company opened a new branch a year ago and the Managing Director at Head Office has asked you to prepare a report on its progress.
- Write your **report** for the Managing Director, including the following information:
  - The reasons for opening the branch;
  - Its successes;
  - Problems experienced;
  - Plans for the coming year.

➤ Question 3

- Your department recently moved to a new building. You are not satisfied with the way the removal company dealt with the move of your furniture and equipment and have decided to write a letter of complaint to the removal company about it.
- Write a **letter** to the removal company, including the following information:
  - Details of the move and what was moved;
  - What was unsatisfactory;
  - What you had expected from the company;
  - What you expect to happen now.

➤ Question 4

- The international organization you work for is considering the possibility of producing a promotional brochure to publicise the company abroad. The Managing Director has asked you to write a contribution for this brochure.
- Write your **proposal** for the Managing Director, including the following information:
  - Possible contents of the brochure;

· Ways to make it attractive;
· Benefits the brochure could have for the company.

Sample answers to Test 4

➤ Question 1

Sample A

Short report: IT expenditure in Europe vs. Asia

The overall result of this international survey on planned IT expenditure for next year shows significant differences between Europe and Asia.

According to the survey results, European companies are almost equally divided between increasing their IT spending, keeping it at this year's level or decreasing it.

The situation in Asia is quite different. Almost 60% of the surveyed Asian companies plan to increase IT expenditure next year, compared to just over a third in Europe.

Finally, the percentage of companies who are planning to keep IT expenditure at the same level is also lower in Asia, although not to the same extent.

Band 5

点评：这是一篇非常优秀的图表习作。首先，作者能够运用简洁的语言，充分地利用图表所提供的信息，出色地完成写作任务，针对欧、亚两地电子产品消费进行了详细的对比分析。其次，该习作作者在语言运用方面也有着良好的把握，语言简洁有力，自然流畅，语法错误极少。例如：第三段的最后一句话，作者能够使用比较复杂的句式充分表达亚洲电子产品的消费不同于欧洲方面。这就很好地体现了作者良好的语言能力。再次，该习作思路清晰，结构严谨，能够恰当地运用各种连接手法。例如："according to; compared to; finally; although"等。最后，文章语言正式，符合商务报告写作特点，且并未出现主观性词汇。

➤ Question 2

Sample B

REPORT ON THE FIRST YEAR OF ACTIVITY OF OUR POLISH SUBSIDIARY

It has been a year now since our new subsidiary called "alpha" opened its doors in Warsaw. Before pointing out its successes, the problems faced and the plans for the coming year, let me remind you the reasons for its opening.

REASONS FOR OPENING

In fact, there was only one main reason for choosing to settle down in Poland: reducing labor cost rates. Indeed, our activity as cosmetics producers requires a lot of staff, and labor costs are much cheaper in Poland than in Switzerland!

SUCCESSES

Knowing this aim, we decided to go on. We managed to build a brand new factory on time, and the line works! That was our greater success: being able to respect the opening date and to produce efficiently.

PROBLEMS EXPERIENCED

However, we met difficulties in two areas:

— transportation: the road's network in Poland is not so good and time spent on transportation is higher than predicted

— staff: we still have a lot to learn about staff's culture and expectations.

PLANS FOR THE COMING YEAR

Our plan for the coming year is mainly to improve the above mentioned points (as production is running quite well). Therefore, we will study the opportunity of buying a few lorries (not to depend on others for delivery). We will also organize seminars for both local staff and overseas managers, to understand each other better.

Finally, I would like to take the opportunity of this report to invite the top management for a visit of alpha, whenever they want.

xx

manager

in charge of the Polish subsidiary

Band 4

点评：这是一篇比较出色的文章。首先能够较好地完成写作任务，内容包括了题中所要求的基本内容。其次，该文章作者能够运用比较流畅的语言来进行较为准确的表达，但其中有少量的语法错误和结构错误，例如在词语搭配、名词所有格的使用以及表达的准确性、时态等方面。此外，作者拥有良好的语言组织能力，注重逻辑性，结构严谨，并能够运用较为复杂的句子。例如作者采用总分的结构来使文章更加清晰明了，尽管在文章的最后运用了“I would like”这样的主观词汇。

➤ Question 3

Sample C

Dear Sirs,

I write to you as a result of the complaints of our company's employees regarding the last weekend's move.

As you well know, the move took place last Saturday and Sunday, the 16th and 17th of November and it involved the movement of 125 pieces of office furniture (including 10 filling cabinets), 80 computers, 10 printers and a fax machine, along with 56 boxes of documents and personal items of the employees.

Unfortunately we are not at all satisfied with your work due to the fact that on Monday morning we found that some of the furniture was damaged and two filling cabinets were missing. Also, most of the boxes were handled incorrectly and, as a result, we found 12 boxes of documents opened and the files placed in the wrong order and some of the personal items got damaged, lost or missplaced.

I find myself very disappointed with the work of your company, especially since you were highly recommended to me as one of the most important removal companies, and I had high expectations regarding the quality of your services.

As for now, I expect your company to try to find the missing items and deliver them as soon as possible and to provide financial compensation for the items that got broken or missplaced. I also expect a reduction on the invoice value since the quality of your services was poor.

Waiting a prompt answer from your company, we remain.

Yours Faithfully

Band 4

点评：这篇习作完成得比较出色。首先，作者能够运用语言较为全面地表达文中所提供的信息，较好地完成了写作任务。其次，在语言的运用方面，我们可以看出作者拥有良好的语言运用能力，但有少量的拼写错误。例如正文第三段和第五段中，“missplaced”应为“misplaced”等。作者能够运用各种连接手法，使文章更具有逻辑性。例如：“as a result; also”等。再次，文章结构比较严谨，安排比较合理，尽管最后未写署名。最后，文章中作者的语气过于强硬，略有不当之处。

➤ Question 4

Sample D

To: The Managing Director

This proposal is for the possibility of producing a promotional brochure to publicise the company abroad.

With globalization and living in the new IT age we have to make known our company in the international market.

The following contents are recommended for the brochure:

- Brief introduction of the company history;
- Range of existing and possible new products;
- Website address;
- List of our clientele and business associates;
- Addresses of our offices located worldwide;
- Sales email contracts/customer services emails contact for interested parties who has inquiry about our products.

We could incorporate more colours and pictures of our products, factory, offices etc. in the brochure. To further enhance its attractiveness we could also attached a CD which will also contain the same information as the brochure and ends with a video clip of the company product—factory processes. We could also consider offering discount or free samples for interested parties who will visit our website address.

This brochure will have a good publicity for the company and most importantly it will create awareness of the company's existence and our range of products and services. I hope you could kindly consider the proposal recommended.

Thank you.

Band 4

点评：这是一篇比较优秀的文章。首先，能够按照要求，比较出色地完成了写作任务，较为全面地表达出了题目中所要求的信息。其次作者具有良好的语言表达能力，语言自然流畅，但有少量的错误，例如表达的准确性以及词语的搭配等方面。再次，作者能够比较恰当地安排语篇，运用了较为复杂的句式，使文章具有良好的逻辑性和严谨性。最后，该习作总体来说也是一篇中性得体的商务写作，尽管在文章中作者使用了“I hope”这样的主观词汇。

Day 5

试题解析与练习（Test 5）

Test 5

WRITING 1 hour 10 minutes

PART ONE

➤ Question 1

- The graph below shows the turnover for three kinds of retail outlet, all owned by the same company, during a three-year period.
- Using the information from the graph, write a short **report** comparing the changes in turnover in the company's three types of outlet.
- Write **120 – 140** words.

PART TWO

Write an answer to **ONE** of the questions 2 – 4 in this part. Write your answer in **200 – 250** words.

➤ Question 2

- Your company would like to break into a new overseas market with your new range of sports goods. You have been asked by Marketing Director to investigate ways of doing this.
- Write your **report** for the Marketing Director, including the following information:
  - How you carried out your research into the market;
  - The existing competition;
  - Your target customers;
  - Ways of promoting the products in the new market.

➤ Question 3

- Recently you have become unhappy with a service that has been provided to your company for a number of years. You have decided to write a letter of complaint to the service provider.
- Write your **letter** to the company that provides the service, including the following information:
  - Which service you are complaining about;
  - Why you are dissatisfied with the service;
  - What action you want the service provider to take;
  - What you will do if there is no improvement in the service.

➤ Question 4

- Your Managing Director is considering how to improve the company's internal communications, and has asked you to write a short proposal giving your views on communication within your department.

- Write the **proposal** for the Managing Director, including the following information:
  - Describing how communication currently takes place within your department;
  - Pointing out the weaknesses of the present situation;
  - Recommending one or two improvements that should be made.

Sample answers to Test 5

➤ Question 1

Sample A

Below is a report on the changes in turnover for three kinds of retail outlet, owned by one company, over a three-year period.

The overall highest turnover of eight million pounds was obtained by supermarkets in 2002. On the other hand, the smallest turnover was made in small shops in 2001.

Over the year 2000, a turnover of fifty million pounds was reached in department stores, whereas it then plummeted to about thirty-five million pounds in 2001 and maintained this position throughout 2002.

The supermarkets turnover rose steadily from 2000, reaching its peak in 2002 with eighty million pounds.

Clearly, small shops had the smallest turnover altogether. Thirty million pounds in 2000, a noticeable drop to twenty million in 2001 and a slight increase of five million in 2002.

In conclusion, the highest results were achieved by supermarkets, followed by department stores and then small shops.

Band 4

点评：该习作能够较好地完成写作任务，属于第四档的作文。从任务完成的角度看，我们不难发现，作者能够完成题目规定的写作任务，并且涵盖了图表中的所有内容。作者不是简单地描述图表上的数字，而是能在观察分析之后，归纳出三种销售门店在不同年份营业额的高低比较结果，例如第二段，并且还能描述某一个特定的零售门店在三年内营业额的增减趋势，例如第四段。在语言上，我们看出作者对词汇和语法有较好的把握，但是文章中也有一些小的错误。比如，第四段“The supermarkets turnover”就出现了语法错误，名词所有格应当在“supermarkets”后边加一个“'”。此外，文章的结构组织也比较合理，首先作者对三个零售门店进行总体比较，然后再分别一一分析每个门店的总体情况，并且文章采用“总分类”的形式。并且在文章中能较合理地运用连接词，例如“whereas；in conclusion”，使得表达流畅，逻辑严谨。

➤ Question 2

Sample B

Report concerning a new overseas market

Introduction

This report sums up the results of my investigation in overseas markets, according to what was demanded by the Marketing Director.

Findings

Staying a few weeks in this part of the World allowed me to collect precious information about the market, buying habits, competitors, and to gather complete figures and statistics.

I could carry out a market research interviewing potentials consumers on the street or even in sports shop. Then I had the opportunity to test local competitors' products and to visit production premises.

Furthermore, I analysed the data and found out two mains competitors, X and Y, who both share half of the total market. The others competitors are small companies representing few percentage of global sales.

Finally, teenagers are the biggest consumers. In fact, 30% of them buy regularly sports articles, while adults declare only buying once a year. Therefore, the main target profile would be a 15-year-old to 25-year-old male.

Conclusions

In my opinion, this market would be a great change for the development of the company and I then recommend breaking into it.

Recommendations

I suggest carrying out an advertisement campaign in order to make them know there is a new competitor. Then consumers are attracted by sales promotion like price reductions and I propose launching our products this way.

Last but not least, we could starting offering three products to the price to two.

Band 3

点评：该习作基本能够完成写作任务，属于第三档的作文。首先作者能够基本完成写作任务，但是有一些任务有所遗漏。此外我们能发现本文中许多的语言错误，例如：在句子 “Furthermore, I analyzed the data and found out two mains competitors, X and Y.” 中，“mains” 后边的 “s” 应当去掉；在句子 “...I propose launching our products this way” 中，正确的句子应当是 “... I propose launching our products in this way.” 诸如此类的语言错误还有很多，但是基本上不太影响读者的理解。另外作者在努力地使用超出自己能力的词汇和表达，但是由于作者对语言的运用能力不是很自如，导致这些表达略显笨拙。例如在 “Introduction” 中，“...according to what was demanded by the Marketing Director.” 作者原本想使用一个宾语从句，但是这种用法导致了表达过于繁琐，反而不如直接使用 “...according to the Marketing Director's demand” 使得表达清晰简洁。最后，这个题目应当要求作者写一个正式的商务报告，但是，在口吻上作者大量地使用 “I could” “I suggest” 等表达，降低了商务报告的客观公正性。其实作者完全可以用被动句或者 “It is suggested that...” 来处理这个习作。

➤ Question 3

Sample C

Dear Mr. Smith,

We have been using your company for a number of years, however, recently we have experienced some problems with the quality of products and delays in delivery.

As our customers have been devotedly visiting our shop for years purchasing the best quality products, we feel obliged to make some remarks.

Not only have we noticed that the date for which dairy products should be consumed was extended but also in some yogurts we found that the labels describing the content were misleading. A cherry yogurt turned out to be a strawberry one. Furthermore, bottles of milk were not sealed properly which resulted in leaking and making the milk go off quicker.

On top of everything, there have been delays in delivery if not a non-delivery that occurred already a few times.

We trust you will give this matter your immediate attention and that everything will get back to normal, as we would still like to use your service. We hope it is just a temporary disposition. Sadly, however, we have to state clearly, that if no improvement will be made both with the quality of items and delivery we will have to change the suppliers, for our customers' sake and our reputation.

Yours Sincerely,

Aneta Mroczek

Band 4

点评：该习作较好地完成了写作任务，是一篇属于第四档的作文。首先作者能够较全面地完成写作任务，涵盖了题目中要求的所有内容。作者使用语言较为自然，表达流畅，词汇使用也较为丰富，能够运用诸如“be obliged to”“result in”“immediate”“temporary”等词汇。在文章的前三段出现了大量的复合句式和较为复杂的表达。例如：在第二段中使用由“as”引导的原因状语从句；第三段中用“Not only...but also”的句式，且在句子中使用了倒装结构。但是值得注意的是，这篇文章中也有一些小的语言缺陷，例如在第一段“We have been using your company...”，此处如果换成“We have cooperated with your company...”则表达会更加准确和地道。最后从这封信的口吻上来看，作者使用的语言也较为谦虚和礼貌，符合题目要求的写作风格。

➤ Question 4

Sample D

Making communication better

We have 10 people working in our admin department. All kind of communication between each other is very important and it needs to be quick and affective. At the moment we do send e-mails for sharing happening in every day basis. We also have a weekly meeting where some of us get together and look over the subjects from previous week and also make plans for the up coming ones. There is also someone there to make notes which will be typed over to correct minutes and sent to everybody who attended the meeting.

My concern is that on those meetings we don't have the whole admin team present and therefore many times we have talked on the behalf of the ones who are not attending. This kind of communication might bring miscommunication to place.

To resolve this matter I think that we should have everybody on that weekly meeting to get correct information from the right people.

At least it is worth to have a go.

Best regards,

Kaie Sirak

Band 2

点评：这是一篇较差的习作，属于第二档。首先，作者不能很好地完成写作任务，遗漏了很多内容，例如在题目中要求作者指出目前公司内部交流存在的问题，但是，作者在第一段中描述了现状之后，并没有在第二段完全指出这些现状所一一对应的问题是哪些，就更谈不上他针对这些问题提出意见了。其次，我们发现在文章中有很多的语言错误，无论是拼写上的还是语法或者搭配上的，这些错误都影响了读者对文章的理解。例如："All kind of communication..." 应该是 "All kinds of communication..." "...in every day basis" "... on the behalf of..." 都是搭配错误；并且第二段第一句话中："My concern is that on those meetings we don't have the whole admin team present..." 就出现了表达错误，如果改成 "It is obvious that there is no need for the whole admin team to attend those meetings" 就能更好一点了。此外，在文中，作者很少使用连接词，这样导致文章的逻辑性不强，前后的衔接不自如。

Day 6

试题解析与练习（Test 6）

Test 6

WRITING 1 hour 10 minutes

PART ONE

➤ Question 1

- The chart below shows the distribution of positive and negative responses given in a market survey about service provision at a leisure centre.
- Using the information from the chart, write a short **report** about the results of the market survey, describing customer reactions to the services provided.
- Write **120 – 140** words.

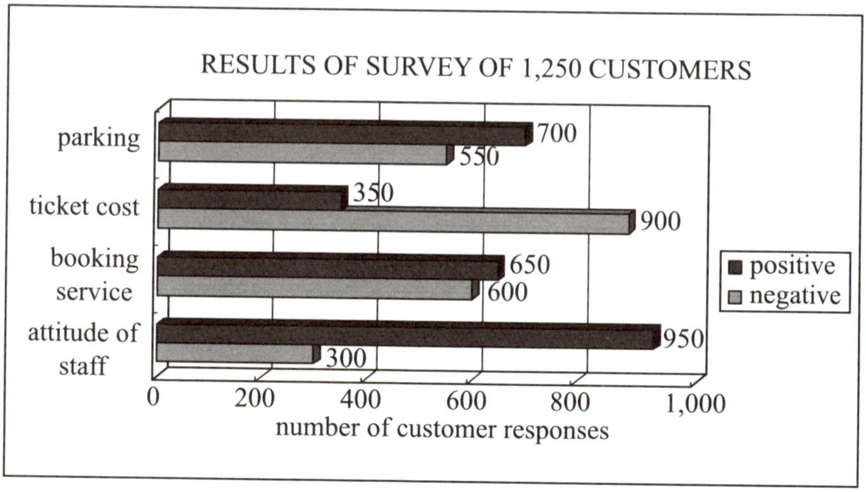

PART TWO

Write an answer to **ONE** of the questions 2 – 4 in this part. Write your answer in **200 – 250** words.

➤ Question 2

- Your company recently sponsored a national event for the first time and your manager has asked you to write a report on this.
- Write your **report** for your manager, including the following information:
  - · A brief description of the event;
  - · Which aspects of the event were particularly successful and why;
  - · The benefits to the company of sponsoring the event;
  - · What needs to be done before considering further sponsorship.

➤ Question 3

- Your company has recently been taken over by another company, and your department has been restructured. This has resulted in a number of problems which you want to make the new owners award of.
- Write a **letter** to the Managing Director of the new owners:
  - · Outlining what the situation in your department was before the takeover;
  - · Explaining what problems have arisen and why;
  - · Suggesting how these problems could be resolved;
  - · Warning what might happen if these problems are not resolved.

➤ Question 4

- Your company's export sales have been falling and the Sales Manger has asked you to consider ways of improving them.
- Write your **proposal** for the Sales Manager:
  - · Giving reasons for the decline in the company's export sales;
  - · Suggesting ways of improving export sales;

· Outlining the additional resources that would be required.

Sample answers to Test 6

➤ Question 1

Sample A

This bar chart shows the number of positive and negative responses given by customers in a market survey about services at a leisure centre.

Asked about the parking facilities at the leisure centre 700 customers responded positively, whereas 550 said something negative about it. Looking at the ticket costs there were almost three times as many people responding negatively than positive. With only 350 positive responses. The booking service was equally evaluated. For this service the survey counted 650 positive and 600 negative responses. In contrast to the ticket costs the attitude of staff was evaluated very positively. Only a fourth of 1, 250 asked customers complained about the attitude of staff. 950 people thought positively about the staff at the leisure centre. Summarising the results of this survey you can say that there is need for improvement in the fields of ticket costs, booking service and parking.

Band 4

点评：该习作较好地完成了写作任务，题目中所列的主要内容都包括在内。作者能够清晰地表达出表格中所体现的全部信息，阐述较为准确。文章对于语言的运用掌握得比较好，能够娴熟地运用动词的分词形式及被动语态，但仍有少量的语法错误，如“a fourth of 1, 250 asked customers”中，“asked”和“customers”是被动关系，应改为“customers asked”才准确。作者对于词汇的使用比较丰富，且用法比较准确。全文布局合理，大量衔接词的运用，如“whereas, in contrast to”都体现了作者较为严谨的文章布局。

➤ Question 2

Sample B

The aim of this report is to give an overview of the event our company decide to sponsor and present the benefits and the pitfalls.

Introduction to the event

"Computer 2003" was the fifth edition of an annual event held in Lausanne (Switzerland). Its goal is to present and promote the innovations in the IT field.

Its success

Designed to inform professionals, the event also reached the interest of the public. During the whole week, the guests took part very actively in the meetings, thereby demonstrating a huge and shared interest, and the public was nothing if not captivated by the demonstrations and shows.

Unfortunately, the opening hours were relatively restrictive and it was therefore really difficult for the visitors to see everything.

The place of our company

As a widely recognized training services provider, we were offered in return of our sponsorship a place to promote our books and training programmes, complemented by advertising areas.

We therefore have been able to reach many potential customers as well as other companies interested in consolidating their staff's knowledge.

The conclusion and expectations of the future

Our company was really well exposed and reached many new potential clients. There is no doubt that our future sales will benefit from the numerous contacts our staff made, and the return on investment is therefore undoubtedly really good and worth our sponsorship.

We should consider this type of action more often. But, as our staff is not used to this type of publicity, we should consider a special training in providing the company and its service before doing this type of action again.

Band 5

点评：该文是一篇非常优秀的分析报告。文中涵盖了题目规定的所有内容，出色地完成了写作任务。作者对于语言的使用熟练自然，能够娴熟地掌握并准确使用同位语从句，定语从句等复杂句式。作者词汇表达非常丰富，一些复杂词汇，如“pitfalls, promote, consolidating, potential”的使用都非常自然精确。文章谋篇布局非常合理，开篇就清晰阐述了本文的写作目的，要点的表述也十分清晰明确。作者还大量运用了衔接词，例如“thereby, unfortunately, therefore”，等等，都体现出了文章精确的逻辑和布局。

➤ Question 3

Sample C

Re: Human Resources Department—restructuring

Dear Mr. Blackwell,

Further to our phone conversation of yesterday, I am writing to detail and explain issues related to the recent restructuring of the HR department. To begin with, I would like to outline what the situation in the department was before the takeover and what has changed since then. Previously led by a local HR manager, our team was handling day-to-day issues and was really open to listen and support employees. Since the take-over, we are now managed by a supervisor who is based in the UK.

As a result, it is difficult to touch base with him on a daily basis and because he's overloaded with his own team in London, it appears that he might not be able to involve himself with the current issues arising within our team.

I fully understand that the restructuring has resulted in increasing the workload in HR but as we are going through severe changes, the staff members need to be supported and guided by a senior manager who could provide them with a legal advice.

Therefore, I suggest organizing weekly team meetings with the new HR manager as well as arranging one-on-ones with each HR member so they can understand what is really expected from them and in which direction this company is going towards.

I think that the above should be seen as a high priority because people tend to feel lost and insecured nowadays and, therefore, don't show a positive attitude.

I look forward to hearing from you.

Best regards,

Eric Marzi

Band 4

点评：该习作较好地完成了写作任务，包括了题目要求的所有内容，表达清晰精练。作者对于语言的掌握能力较强，对于简单句、复合句以及时态的把握比较自然准确。但文中也存在着一些错误，如对于完成时态的表述上。值得一提的是，文章中使用了大量的被动语态，且使用较为准确。文章用词比较丰富，结构布局合理，使用了较多的衔接词，如"to begin with, as a result, therefore"等。本文比较符合信件的格式与写作习惯。

➤ Question 4

Sample D

Objective: Export Sales Decline Analysis

Introduction

The aim of this report is to bring to management attention the causes of the dramatic sales decline over the last 3 quarters.

Findings

As all of us are aware that the main reason for this sharp collapse can be found in two different problems: the first, the devaluation of US dollars; the second, an inefficient sales force and, in particular an incompetent export manager incapable of motivating the staff. While the first issue can be addressed with a more accurate analysis of the prices of our products the second will require a swift management decision in order to restructure the organization.

Recommendation and Conclusion

In order to address the first issue, it is mandatory that management delegates more power to the CFO in order to adjust our prices to the new exchange rate on a regular basis. On the organization side, on the contrary, managent will be required to appoint a new export manager with more initiative and motivated to rebuild the entire staff.

Of course all this will require an additional investment of resources and some quarters of negative sales. In particular recruiting a new export manager will require an accurate selection process and an integration plan of a couple of months before tangible results can be seen. However I'm confident that the change will be extremely beneficial in energizing a very demotivated sales force.

Band 4

点评：这是一篇比较好的习作。文章涵盖了题目所列出的主要内容，要点阐述非常明确。作者布局较为合理，开篇提出本文的写作目的，然后分点陈述，结构非常清晰，并且对于语言的运用能力也比较强，文中对于复合句的使用较为准确、恰当。但作者对于比较级的使用仍稍欠妥当，如“a new export manager with more initiative and motivated to...”中，从结构一致上看“more”后面要跟名词，因此应用“motivation”而不是“motivated”。总体来讲，除了最后一段使用了比较主观性的短语，如“I'm confident that...”等，该文仍是一篇比较中性得体的商务报告。

Day 7

试题解析与练习（Test 7）

Test 7

WRITING 1 hour 10 minutes

PART ONE

➤ **Question 1**

- The three charts below show a company's operating profit (in $ million), turnover (in $ million) and unit sales (i. e. number of products sold) in the three years 2001 – 2003.
- Using the information from the charts, write a short **report** describing the company's performance in the three years.
- Write **120 – 140** words.

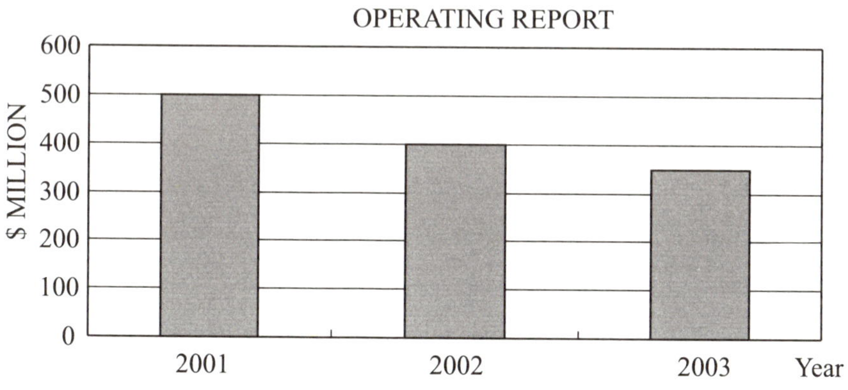

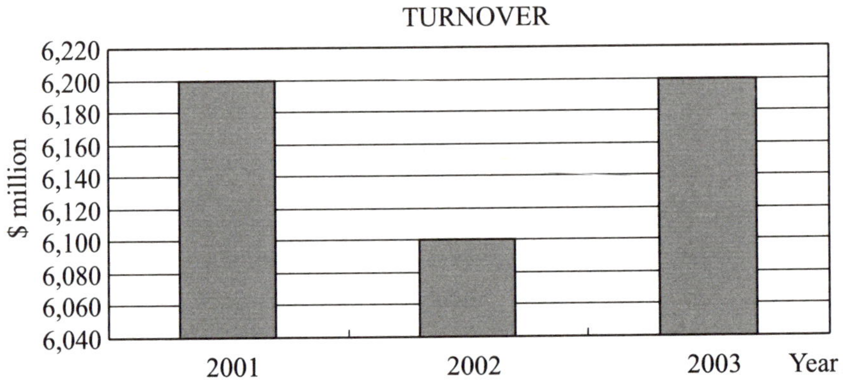

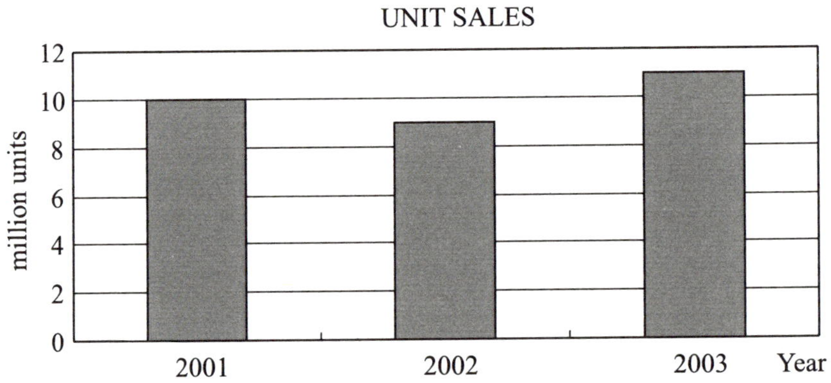

PART TWO

Write an answer to **ONE** of the questions 2 – 4 in this part. Write your answer in **200 – 250** words.

➤ Question 2

- You work for a supermarket chain and have been asked by the board of directors to write a report on a site where the company is considering building a new supermarket.
- Write your **report** for the board, including the following information:
  · A description of the site, including its location;
  · The advantages and disadvantages of the sites;
  · Your opinion as to whether the site is suitable.

➤ Question 3

- A company you already do business with has recently created a new product line. Your department placed an order for the new product, but found that the product did not fulfill your requirements and that the after-sales service was poor. Your head of department has asked you to write a letter to the company informing them of your dissatisfaction.
- Write a **letter**, including the following information:
  - · What the order was for and when it was placed;
  - · Why you are dissatisfied with both the product and the after-sales service;
  - · A reminder of business done with them in the past;
  - · What you expect in response to your complaint.

➤ Question 4

- Your company has recently experienced a drop in sales, and your Managing Director has asked you to write a short proposal about improving the advertising of your company's products or services.
- Write your **proposal** for the Managing Director:
  - · Commenting on the effectiveness of the advertising you are currently using;
  - · Recommending one or two changes to your advertising;
  - · Explaining how these changes would affect sales.

Sample answers to Test 7

➤ Question 1

Sample A

<u>Performance Report 2001 – 2003</u>

<u>Introduction</u>

The aim of this report is to describe the company's performance in the years 2001 –

2003.

2001

In 2001 the company's turnover was at its peak and the operating profit reached the 500 million dollar mark. They sold 10 million units what was the reason for this excellent result.

2002

In the following year, the company had to handle a decrease in operating profits of 20% as well as a decline of their turnover, which was a result of less units which were sold.

2003

In 2003, the company was able to sell more units again, so they could increase their turnover but their operating profits still went down, because they had to pay the last year's failure.

Conclusion

The company's performance was great in 2001 and 2003, just in 2002 they had little problems because of a decrease of their units sold. The company won't have problems in the future.

Band 3

点评：该篇习作基本完成了题目中要求的写作任务。文章结构比较清晰，但文章的表达欠佳，词汇的运用相对有限，并且有词汇和语法错误，例如："they sold 10 million units what was the reason for this excellent result" 中使用了错误的关系词，"little problems" 中的修饰词使用不正确。从整体上看，是一篇合格的文章。

➤ Question 2

Sample B

The aim of this report is to decide the consideration of building a new supermarket.

Description

At first I'll make a short description of the site. The location of the planed supermarket is very close to the city centre and surrounded by lot of smaller shops. Concerning the infrastructure it is very well located because it can be reached by nearly all means of transport.

Advantages

As I already mentioned, the infrastructure is very good and you have good connections of public means of transport. Another positive aspect for building the supermarket is the competition. Our supermarket can offer much cheaper prices than all the surrounding little shops so we are very competitive.

Disadvantages

The first thing I want to put forward is that it is very cost intensive to set up a new supermarket in this area because the land prices are very high. The second disadvantage which I want to point out is that there is not enough space for parking and might be very expensive to build a garage under the building.

Personal opinion

To summarise, it is a very expensive location with less space for building a parking area but you have good chances for getting a high profit in the long term. Although there are a lot of smaller shops nearby the supermarket, there is no doubt in being the most competitive!

Finally I think that this will be a very profitable location for building a new supermarket.

Band 4

点评：本文语言运用得体，结构布局清晰，能够完成题目中要求的任务，并且能够正确使用一些句型，如："it is found that, as I already mentioned"。因此，从整体上看是一篇较好的习作。但当中也不乏一些语法和词汇搭配错误，例如："is very close to the city centre and surrounded by lots of smaller shops"当中错误地省略了主语，"cheaper prices"搭配不当。此外，语言风格的使用不完全恰当，作为一篇书面报告不应该出现较为口语化的表达方式。

➤ Question 3

Sample C

15 May, 2004

Dear Sir,

We have received your products, but we are very sorry that your products don't meet our requirements and your after-sales service is not satisfactory.

We placed the order on April 20, in which we had expressed our detailed instructions. As our customers requested, we ordered your new refrigerators by one thousand with the size of two by one by one metre. We believed that you could send us the right products as you used to. To our great disappointment, we found that the refrigerators are bigger than what we want. We have received a large number of complaints from our customers for this.

We think that it is understandable that there may be something wrong with the new product line, but your after-sales service really lets us down. We have contacted you for this problem and seeked for a solution. However, you responded slowly to our enquiry and your explanation and solution are not reasonable.

We have been good business partners since we established business relation two years ago. We are always satisfactory with your offerings and after-sales service. We are greatly impressed with your excellent quality and quick delivery. We believe you will continue to do so.

We hope that you can give us a reasonable explanation as soon as possible, and most importantly, recall these refrigerators you have sent us, and deliver one thousand refrigerators to our specification within four weeks.

Best regards,

Elaine White

Band 3

点评：这篇文章基本上完成了题目中所要求的任务，内容表达基本充分。结构组织比较清晰，整体而言，是一篇合格的习作。短语运用较得当，例如："as our customers requested" "to our great disappointment"。但是文章中有不少的语法和词汇使用错误，如："we found that the refrigerators are bigger than what we want." 中主从句时态不一致，第三段中的时态使用比较混乱，给读者的理解造成了一些困难。

➤ Question 4

Sample D

Introduction

The aim of this proposal is to analyse the recent drop in sales in one of our oversea branches and then to propose feasible ways to promote the sales there.

Findings

It is found that our new-launched product—chocolate pie enjoyed a favourable market at the beginning of the campaign. However, the sales began to decline recently according to the figures presented by Sales Department. It is said that there are several factors cause the current situation but the main reason is the failure in the advertising we are currently using.

At first the advertising did work, the jingle is easy to remember and the stereotype we focused is funny, therefore, it was popular with local residents. However, as time goes by, the passion for it is gone, too. The survey shows that people began to feel it was too exaggerated and even a little bit hostile. And this leads directly to the refusion of purchasing our product.

Recommandations

We strongly recommend that we should cancel all the present TV commercials and launch a new one. And this time we should make it compatible with local taste so as to generate sales and more importantly to improve our company's image in the local market. If possible we can also invite some local stars to endorse our product which may change their negative attitude on the previous advertisement.

Band 4

点评：

该习作较好地完成了写作任务。尽管某些地方少量语言不确切，作者运用了丰富的词汇与句型结构。文章结构清晰，运用了一些衔接手段。

Week 5
靶向演练

Day 1

TEST 1

PART ONE

➤ Question 1

- The pie charts below show the means of transport used by city dwellers in China in 1988 and 2008.
- Using the information from the charts, write a short **report** concerning the changes.
- Write **120 – 140** words.

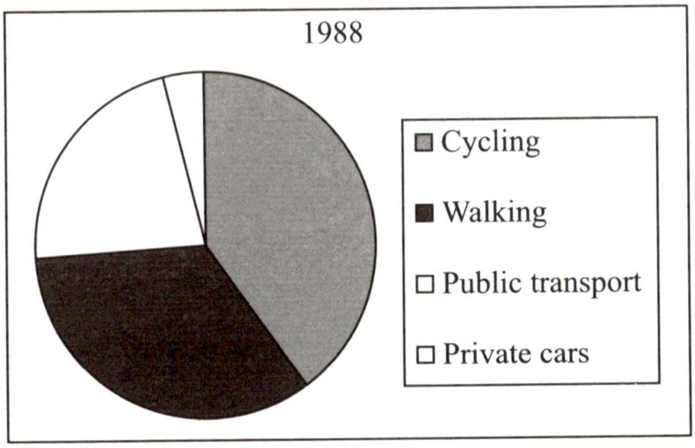

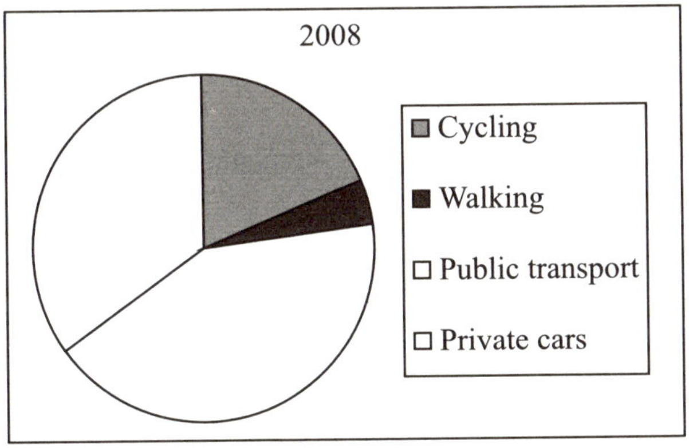

PART TWO

Questions 2 – 4

- Write an answer to **one** of the questions 2 – 4 in this part.
- Write **200 – 250** words on pages 5 and 6.
- Write the question number in the box at the top of page 5.

➤ Question 2

- Your manager is keen to improve work efficiency among the staff. He has asked you to introduce to your fellow staff members practices to improve time management
- Write the **report** for your manager, including the following information:
  - · The importance of planning work time effectively;
  - · Practices to improve time management;
  - · Steps to follow in carrying out the practices.

➤ Question 3

- One of your company's products is suffering from downturn in sales recently. You think that an advertising campaign will help increase sales.
- Write a **letter** to the Managing Director
  - · Explaining why you think an advertising campaign would help;
  - · Stating the cost of the advertising campaign;
  - · Predicting how it would help the sales of the product.

➤ Question 4

- The IT company you work for is thinking about acquiring one of the Telecommunications Company. You have been asked to do some research about it and write a proposal.
- Write your **proposal**, including the following:
  - · Identifying which company to acquire;
  - · Explaining the advantages of acquiring that company;
  - · Suggesting the steps to follow in the acquisition;

· Discussing the risks involved in the acquisition.

练习参考答案

PART ONE

➤ Question 1

Report on the Transport Means in China

Introduction

This report presents the changes in the adoption of transport means by city dwellers in China over the 20 years between 1988 and 2008.

Findings

The above two pie charts reflect the changes of Chinese dwellers' transport means over the 20 years between 1988 and 2008. Generally speaking, in 1988, the majority adopted cycling and walking as the major transportation means, with their percentages being 40% and 34% respectively. However, the proportions of these two means have dropped drastically, by 2008, to 19% and 4%.

On the other hand, the most notable increase is the number of private cars whose percentage increased from 4% in 1988 to 35% in 2008. Similarly, public transport also became a commonly adopted means of transport whose proportion increased by 20%.

PART TWO

➤ Question 2

To: Roger Brown

From: Will Smith

Date: Oct. 23, 2009

Subject: Time Management

Introduction

I am happy to be tasked with this report on improving our work efficiency. I am with you that we are not highly efficient due to the fact that we do not manage our time well. I still remember a famous saying that "Time passes very fast, however, it is fair to everybody, not giving one a second more, and also not giving others one second less. It all depends on how you can make use of it." Therefore, if we can improve our skills of time management, we could do our work punctually, efficiently, and also easily.

Recommendations

There are many ways of helping us manage our time. The greatest way to do this is to get everybody to have their daily, weekly, and even monthly work plan. As a result, we will need to look at our yearly performance objectives, and break it into a monthly plan, i. e. , we will need to complete a certain task within this month. People can personally decide on which date they prefer to work on this. To manage time also means that we will need to deal with interruptions. I would recommend to our people that we deal with them, but also we need to bear in mind our priorities, our monthly and yearly target. If they have trouble balancing them, I suggest that they let you make decisions for them.

The calendar function of Microsoft Office Inbox can help people to plan their time. They will be advised to put in calendar their planned work and task, and also open their calendar among the team so that we can take a look and see if they are doing it well or not.

➤ Question 3

Dear Mr. Green,

I am writing about the recent downturn in the selling of the tape-recorder C100, which has brought us a lot of profits over the past 10 years.

Recently CD players have been selling very well, which partly leads to the decline of the selling of our C100. If we still do nothing about it, possibly the sales of C100 will continue to fall. In view of the present situation, I think we should put up roadshows near primary schools and high schools since students have long remained our loyal customers. We have to make it clear that if they want to listen to English tapes or songs, C100 is their best choice because it not only has the best sound quality and also the coolest image.

Since we will only need to put up some posters and our own staff could be in the roadshows, I do not think we have to invest very much in it. The point is, we have to design the most appealing posters and the best slogans to convey to the prospective customers that we are always leading the fashion. And we could give the person who buys on the spot a 5% to 10% discount, and this may help selling a lot.

Yours Sincerely,

Will Smith

➤ Question 4

Introduction

This proposal sets out to make some suggestions as to acquiring one of the Telecommunications Company.

Findings

After we have done careful research, we find that there are a lot of advantages of acquiring AirTouch. First of all, AirTouch Telecommunications Company is a very famous foreign company in the related industry. Once the acquisition is successful, in the short run we could not only expand the company and easily enter a new market, but also complement a product porfolio to satisfy our clients. In the long run, by reducing cost, we can seize a bigger market share and raise share value. As can be imagined, it will surely make a great profit.

Recommendations

In the process of acquisition, we had better follow some rules and steps. Generally speaking, our co-operation is a capital-acquisition contract, which means that we must figure out which side has the primary power to run the company acquired. Respecting our partner's strength, our company still has the right to make a strategic decision for the further growth of the company acquired.

Conclusion

Although there are great potential profits and possible competitive edges in acquisition, the risks involved cannot be ignored. For instance, between two companies with different national cultures, there may be a destructive cultural conflict. Furthermore, the redundancy phenomenon may be very serious.

Day 2

TEST 2

PART ONE

➤ Question 1

- The graph below shows the expenses on fast food by Chinese teenagers.
- Using the information from the graph, write a short **report** concerning the changes.
- Write **120 – 140** words.

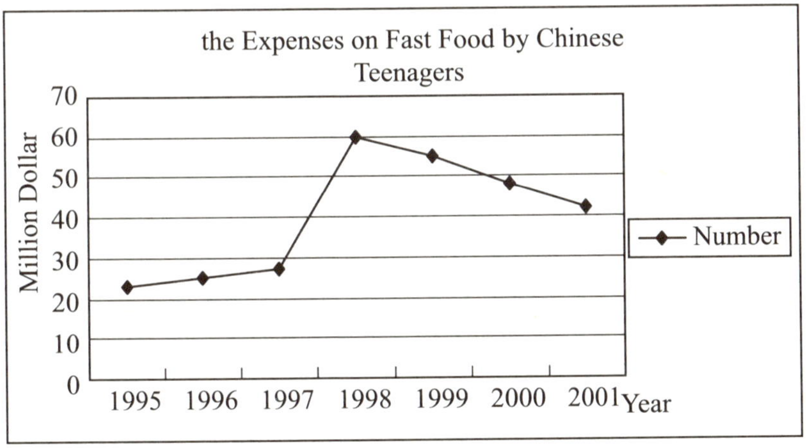

PART TWO

Questions 2 – 4

- Write an answer to **one** of the questions 2 – 4 in this part.
- Write **200 – 250** words on pages 5 and 6.
- Write the question number in the box at the top of page 5.

➤ Question 2

- Your manager is planning to improve relations with customers. He has asked you to write a report about ways to make customers feel valued.
- Write the **report** for your manager, including the following information:
  · The current relations with customers;
  · What practices could be adopted to improve customer relations;
  · How our company could benefit from it.

➤ Question 3

- Your company has put an advertisement on a local newspaper to recruit a manager for an overseas subsidiary, an applicant has written to show interest in it.
- Write a **letter** to the applicant;
  · Introducing your corporate culture to him;
  · Defining the job responsibilities;
  · Terms and conditions of employment, etc.

➤ Question 4

- Your company has decided to concentrate more on establishing employee loyalty. The Managing Director has asked you to do some research and write a proposal about it
- Write your **proposal**, including the following:
  · A brief outline of the current state of employee loyalty;
  · Some possible measures to establish staff loyalty;
  · The possible outcomes of the measures;
  · Possible risks involved in the measures.

练习参考答案

PART ONE

➤ Question 1

Report on Chinese Teenagers' Expenses on Fast Food

Introduction

This report shows the fluctuation of Chinese teenagers' expenses on fast food over half a dozen years from 1996 to 2001.

Findings

As is manifested in the above graph, the expenses of Chinese teenagers on fast food experienced fluctuated over the 6 years in question.

From 1995 to 1997 the total amount that Chinese teenagers spend on fast food drastically increased from 23 million to 27 million USD; thereafter, in the following year, the rise continued and reached its peak, 60 million USD; from 1998, the total amount gradually dropped and the expenses went back to 42 million USD in the year 2001.

PART TWO

➤ Question 2

To: Roger Brown

From: Will Smith

Date: Oct. 23, 2009

Subject: Customer Relations Improvement

Introduction

The recent customers' satisfaction survey shows that our customers satisfaction rate is 58%, which is comparatively lower than the market average 65%, as advised by our marketing competitiveness consultant. Generally speaking, we are good at market rate, delivery time, and the issues that our customers are concerned with are flexibility in paying.

Findings

Currently we do not allow any flexibility in our customers pay time and amount. This saves our energy to manage our account. However, some of our long-term and valued customers would think that their need is not addressed. My recommendation to this is that for those customers that are with us for 3 years and above, and those customers whose purchasing volumes are larger than 20 tons per month, we can give favorable terms of 40 days other than 30 days.

Conclusion

This may slightly influence our cash flow. However, this is worth doing. It will only be applicable to our customers with good credit. This is our first step in differentiating the customers. This will make them feel that we treasure them, address to their needs, and also would like to provide support in their way of development. I believe that they would be stable and with us longer.

➤ Question 3

Dear Mr. Green,

We have received your letter enquiring about the details of the recruitment. Thanks for your interest in our company and your application for a post as a manager for an overseas subsidiary.

Our company has a history of nearly 150 years and enjoys high fame as a high quality coffee producer. We advocate fairness, harmony and humanity. Our corporate culture is that all the employees have a role in the management and each of us is trying our best to make a contribution to the company's progress.

The manager's position is of vital importance for the future and further development of our subsidiary. First of all, the applicant should possess the ability to quickly have the overall situation under his control and to handle urgent matters. And as the head of the company not only does he have to know how to use talents, making the applicants serve our company better, but also learns to unite them as a team invigorated with fighting power. It will be very satisfying if the applicant has compelling experience related to this post.

Once an applicant is chosen, we will provide very satisfactory pay, a substantial salary, good welfare and comfortable working conditions.

Please do not hesitate to contact me if you need any further questions.

Yours sincerely,

Will Smith

➤ Question 4

Introduction

This proposal aims at showing why employee loyalty has deteriorated and suggesting ways of improving the current situation.

Current Situation

A survey among the employees has shown the low employee loyalty. The key findings are outlined as follows:

Unsatisfactory salaries and not enough fringe benefits are some of the real reasons for this problem It is generally felt that the company's competitors offer higher levels of remuneration.

There appears to be a lack of information and resources needed for employees to do a good job. They also lack the necessary skills to meet the requirement of the job.

Measures

We strongly recommend the following measures:

Carry out a review of the current salary structure involving comparison with similar organization.

Provide regular and specific information and resources to employees based on the requirements. Also ensure, through ongoing training, that employees acquire the necessary expertise to fulfill their responsibilities.

Possible Outcomes

By these measures we can undoubtedly establish employee loyalty and they will have a positive impact on the performance of the company.

Possible Risks

The possible risks, if these measures are adopted, are that they are quite time consuming and this of course will lead to more costs. But a high turnover will be more rewarding.

Day 3

TEST 3

PART ONE

➤ Question 1

- The graph below shows the number of TV watchers in China.
- Using the information from the graph, write a short **report** describing the situation.
- Write **120 – 140** words.

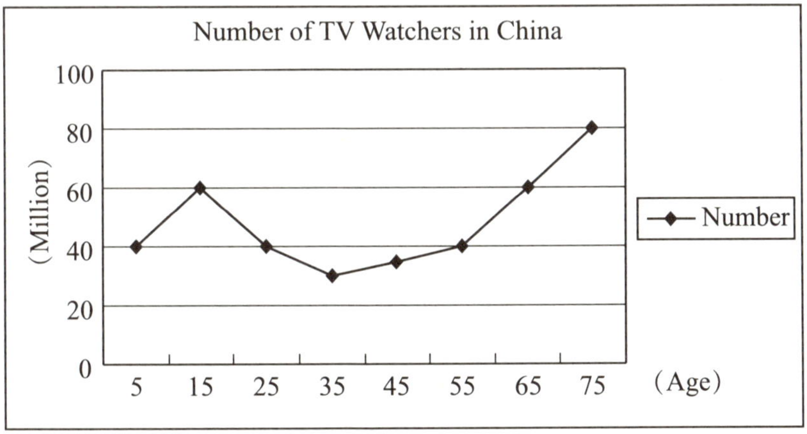

PART TWO

Questions 2 – 4

- Write an answer to **one** of the questions 2 – 4 in this part.
- Write **200 – 250** words on pages 5 and 6.
- Write the question number in the box at the top of page 5.

➤ Question 2

- Your company is planning to promote the sales of a product. You have been asked to do some research concerning whether to give a discount or to launch an advertising campaign.

- Write the **report** for the Sales Manager, concerning:
  · The sales of the product for the last 3 months;
  · Which of the two practices you would adopt;
  · What benefits it will bring about.

➤ Question 3

- A customer has returned a digital camera for it was the wrong model as a result of a mistake in packing. You are asked by your manager to write a letter to give a response
- Write a **letter** to the customer:
  · Apologizing for the mistake;
  · Explaining how the mistake was made;
  · Suggesting several compensation methods.

➤ Question 4

- Your company is looking for a manager for the Accounting Department. You have been asked to do some research concerning whether to promote internally or recruit from outside
- Write your **proposal**, including the following:
  · An analysis of the corporate culture;
  · Which of the two practices is more in line with the corporate culture;
  · Benefits that will be brought with your proposal;
  · Possible risks involved in the practice.

练习参考答案

PART ONE

➤ Question 1

Introduction

This graph shows the number of TV watchers of different age groups in China.

Findings

There is a very small number of TV watchers in China at age 5, 25 and 45, which is approximately 40 million. In contrast, the number of 15 year old TV watchers goes up to 60 million. However, there is a sharp fall from 60 million fifteen year old TV watchers to 30 million thirty-five year old TV watchers. It could be seen that there is a steady increase in the number of people over forty-five year old who watch TV. The highest number is reached at 80 million for 75 year olds.

PART TWO

➤ Question 2

To: Roger Brown

From: Will Smith

Date: Oct. 23, 2009

Subject: Advertising Campaign

Introduction

This report aims to probe how an advertising campaign can help promote the sales of a product.

Findings

Compared with the same time period in last year, our sales volume remains stable in the last 3 months. This is not at all satisfactory as we target to achieve 5% increment in the yearly sales volume. Such stability will stop us from doing so. Therefore, I propose that an advertising campaign be taken to change this.

Recommendations

Two ways of advertising are recommended based on the current situation. First, we can organize promotion activities, i. e. , add 100 you get the second piece free on our counters in the big Dept. stores. This is attractive to the regular customers, and they will be happy to bring their relatives and friends to us. The second approach is targeted at the corporate purchase for the coming Chinese traditional Spring Festival. We will design a special package for the whole-sale to those companies who purchase annual gifts to the employees, and customers.

Conclusion

The 2 approaches are targeted either at the individual or the corporate purchase, and this will help increase the sales volume, and also reduce our storage, improve the cash flow of the company. This will in the end get us to achieve the 5% increment in the sales volume over last year.

➤ Question 3

Dear Mr. Green,

We are extremely sorry to learn that you have received a wrong model of our digital camera and we sincerely apologize to you for the mistake we have made.

In actuality, we have to admit that a mistake was made in packing. We have conducted an investigation concerning your complaint and have found that an employee made a careless mistake while he continued working while he had caught a cold for he had a big family to provide for. We hope you can understand his situation and although we greatly regret for the inconvenience caused.

I have written to our manager about it and he has suggested two ways for compensation to you. If you would like to keep the current model, we intend to arrange a discount of 10% in this purchase as compensation although there is no price difference between the two models and you can get the discount in cash immediately at your confirmation. Or we can exchange the old camera for the right model for you immediately.

We hope you will continue to show interest in our products and support us. I sincerely hope that you will accept our apologies.

Yours sincerely,

Will Smith

➤ Question 4

Introduction

This proposal is concerned with the appointment of a manager for the Accounting Department. I consider that our company should recruit from outside rather than promote internally.

Findings

Research shows that we had better hunt for a manager from outside. First of all, our company has always advocated passion and energy. As long as we could pour into fresh elements by recruiting some new employees, our company may possess the power to make further development. Therefore, recruiting from outside is more in line with the corporate culture. It has a profound meaning for our company's improvement.

Recommendations

As a matter of fact, we could advertise in the local and national newspapers for an accounting manager, and then arrange interviews. There will be many benefits in employing a proficient manager from outside. He or she not only can bring in new precious experience, but also can challenge some stereotyped modes of business operation. Where there is change, there is progress.

Conclusions

However, there is no denying that some possible risks are involved. Anyone who has not worked in our company can not understand our company's culture from the start. He or she may need some time to adapt to the circumstances.

Day 4

TEST 4

PART ONE

➤ Question 1

- The graph below shows the number of coffee drinkers in the U. S. A. and that in China.
- Using the information from the graph, write a short **report** describing the general movement.
- Write **120 – 140** words.

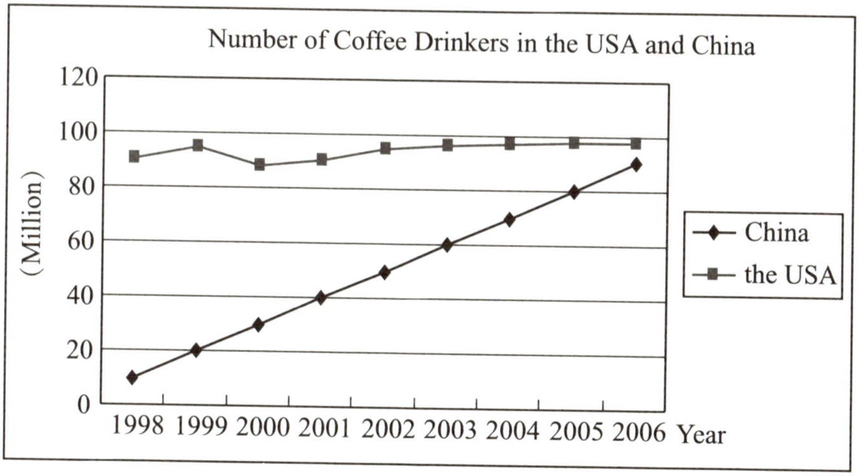

PART TWO

Questions 2 – 4

- Write an answer to **one** of the questions 2 – 4 in this part.
- Write **200 – 250** words on pages 5 and 6.
- Write the question number in the box at the top of page 5.

➤ Question 2

- The Human Resources Manager of your company is planning to offer the staff some training courses. You have been asked to do a survey concerning the courses offered.
- Write the **report** for the Human Resources Manager, including the following information:
  - · Identifying two courses that will be most useful for the general staff;
  - · Explaining the benefits of the courses;
  - · Giving reasons why these courses would be useful.

➤ Question 3

- The secretary to the Personnel Manager of a company has written to you saying that her company is planning to ask you to offer the course to 50 employees. Write her a letter giving her more information about the course.
- Write a letter to the Personnel Manager:
  - · Introducing details about the course;
  - · Telling the arrangements for giving them the training;
  - · Stating the price and requirements.

➤ Question 4

- Your company is planning to launch a new mode of cellphone. You have been asked to do some research and put forward a proposal.
- Write your **proposal**, including the following:
  - · When and where to launch the cellphone;
  - · Promotion activities to go with the launch;
  - · Possible benefits that the launch will bring to the company;
  - · Possible risks involved.

练习参考答案

PART ONE

➤ Question 1

Introduction

This report shows the numbers of coffee drinkers in the U. S. A. and that in China between 1998 and 2006.

Findings

As can be seen from the graph the number of coffee drinkers in USA does not change much, which is around 90 million, from 1998 to 2006. And there is a slight rise from 2002 to 2006, reaching the peak of 100 million. As for that in China, the number increases gradually from 10 million to nearly 100 million over the eight years. In the year 2006 the number of coffee drinkers in China is nearly as much as that in the United States of America.

PART TWO

➤ Question 2

To: Roger Brown

From: Will Smith

Date: Oct. 23, 2009

Subject: Training Courses

Introduction

This report aims to suggest what courses to be offered to our employees.

Findings

The survey concerning the training courses offered to the employees has been completed, and the return rate of the survey is 79% which is very good already. The result of the survey shows that 56% of the staff are interested in internal training courses, rather than going outside. Among the 8 training courses that we are considering, 45% of the people think highly of the Communication Skills Training and Business Acumen Training.

Recommendations

These 2 courses are developed by an international training organization who is well-known in our industry. They know what the industry people need and also what problems and issues that should be addressed. The Communication Skills courses are targeted to improve people's way of interacting with each other, and this will help improve work efficiency, and the morale of the people. The Business Acumen one is targeted to give people the knowledge of the business, the industry, and the development trend, so that people are ready for any of the change, and make it an opportunity for us.

Conclusion

As a new company of 2 years, the two courses will help our people to align with each other both in the soft skills, and also business understanding. We will be aligned to stride in the direction that we should go.

➤ Question 3

Dear Ms. Green,

Thank you for your letter concerning the course Managing Time to your employees.

This is one of the most popular courses and most participants find this course rewarding and insightful. A lot of companies ask us to give this course to their staff at various levels separately, for the employees on different levels have different responsibilities.

You tell me that you plan to put 50 people in the course, and we put a maximum of 30 people in a course. As a result, we plan to divide your employees into two groups according to their job responsibilities and offer the course two times.

This is a two day course and after the three half-day lectures for each course we have a half day presentation from the participants who report how they reorganize their time and their job responsibilities. The participant who has made the most scientific design in his group will get a reward. Since you have two groups to attend the course, we will arrange the course on the first two days and the last two days of the first week of December since as you tell me you do not want the course on Wednesday when you have conferences.

I would like you to put the fifty two into two groups and email us the arrangement. An OHP and a microphone are all we need for the lecture. If you have any further questions, please do not hesitate to ask.

Yours Sincerely,

Will Smith

➤ Question 4

Introduction

The purpose of this proposal is to recommend the time and location to launch our new mode of cell phone and to suggest ways of promotion.

When and Where

Time: Since the target customers of our new mode of cell phone are students, the summer holiday will be the best promotion time when new college students are leaving home and have to purchase cell phones to communicate with their family.

Place: the Victory Shopping Mall located near the campus is our best choice, as the square in front of the mall has enough space for the launch and around the mall there are a dozen universities.

How and What

We strongly recommend the following promotion activities:

Promotional flyers: We should create quality promotional flyers that tell consumers of the advanced quality and competitive price of our product. It should also include our key features and after sales services.

Promotional video: Simple, short-length product demonstration videos are real eye-catchers. In the video we can show that our cell phone can be used everywhere in the world.

Coupons: Most consumers love coupons and a $ 10 coupon can stimulate sales of our new cell phone.

Possible Benefits

These promotion methods will help gain success for the new product and as a result have a positive impact on the image of the company.

Possible Risks

The possible risks, if there are some, of these promotions are that it rains a lot in summer and on a rainy day maybe there will not be many participants. Therefore, we should pay attention to weather forecast and prepare for a rainy day.

Day 5

TEST 5

PART ONE

➤ Question 1

- The **graph** below shows the number of college students studying science in China.
- Using the information from the graph, write a short **report** describing the trend.
- Write **120 – 140** words.

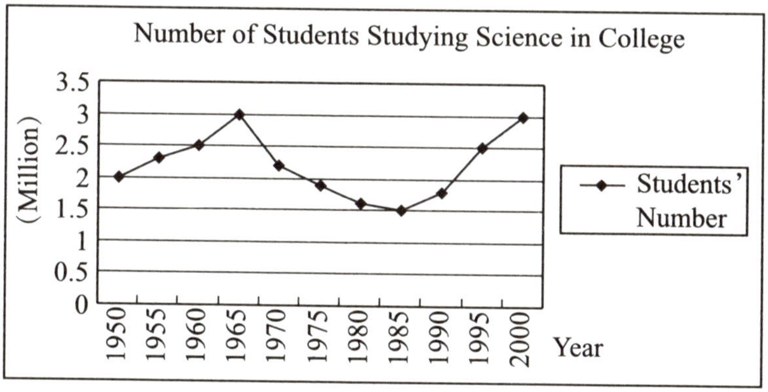

PART TWO

Questions 2 – 4

- Write an answer to **one** of the questions 2 – 4 in this part.
- Write **200 – 250** words on pages 5 and 6.
- Write the question number in the box at the top of page 5.

➤ Question 2

- The Head of Marketing in your company is looking for a tourist resort for the staff in his department to spend the holiday. You have been asked by the manager to do some research.

- Write the **report** for your manager, including the following information:
  - Identifying a place to spend the holiday;
  - The positive and negative aspects of the place as a tourist resort;
  - How the staff of the Marketing Department could benefit from spending a holiday there.

➤ Question 3

- A local company has advertised for an Accounting Manager. You would like to apply for the position and would like to know more about that position.
- Write a **letter** of application to the Personnel Manager;
  - Introducing yourself and your credentials;
  - Getting further information about the position;
  - Stating your expectations.

➤ Question 4

- A group of business people from a foreign trade delegation are visiting your company next month. You have been asked to help prepare a program of activities for the visitors.
- Write your **proposal**, including the following:
  - What kinds of activities would be suitable for the visitors;
  - Which company personnel the visitors should meet;
  - How to entertain the visitors outside working hours.

练习参考答案

PART ONE

➤ Question 1

Introduction

The aim of this report is to describe the change over fifty years in the number of college students studying science in China.

Findings

Between 1950 and 1965, there is a slight rise from 2 million to 3 million college students studying science in China. However, after the year 1965, the number plummeted and until 1985 the number of science students in college reached a record low of 1.5 million. Following the sharp increase, the number goes back to 2.5 million in 1995 and then further back to 3 million in 2000, which comes up to the historical record that is reached in 1965.

PART TWO

➤ Question 2

To: Roger Brown
From: Will Smith
Date: Oct. 23, 2009
Subject: Tourist Resort

Introduction

This report aims to suggest the tourist resort we go to for the annual away days from the company.

Recommendations

For the annual away days from the company for Marketing Dept, I will propose that we go to Zhaoqing Tianmu Hills and Hot Spring Resort. It is the most feasible plan with both the time limits and our budget plan, and I am sure that our people will enjoy going there.

Zhaoqing Tianmu Hills and Hot Spring Resort is developed by a famous Hong Kong tour company, and is managed now by the renowned inter-continental hotel management group. Other than the green hills, lavender field, recreation facilities, drifting, and hot spring, it is now providing teambuilding activities for us. The only disadvantage of the resort is that it is 5 hours' drive away. My solution to this is that we leave on Friday after we complete work, and stay two nights there. We can have this within our budget.

Conclusion

The resort is good place, and the facilities are quite new. We can have our people relax there to go to hot spring, and also have them active by attending the team building activities they offer free of charge. It will be definitely a both relaxing and active holiday.

➤ Question 3

Dear Mr. Green,

I have seen your advertisement for an Accounting Manager in today's newspaper and would like to apply for it.

Although I am currently working in the Accounting Department of a large multinational company, I would appreciate to work for a rapidly expanding young company such as yours, for I really love challenges.

As you can see from my enclosed CV, I got my bachelor's dgree with honors in Accounting from Peking University in 2000. In college I thoroughly enjoyed life and research and gained invaluable insights into the nature of accounting. After leaving university I initially spent time working for a small local firm before finding my current job as assistant to the Accounting Manager and I feel that I am more suited to the dynamics and varied demands of a smaller firm. I possess not only rich work experience, but also great enthusiasm for anything new. As a result, I feel that I would be able to undertake the duties as an Accounting Manager.

I hope I will be paid higher than I used to for I am shouldering more responsibilities and if I could be given more flexibility in the management of my time I will be very happy.

I am available for interview from 15 October and I can clarify the information in the CV if you are interested in my education and previous and present employment.

I look forward to hearing from you.

Yours sincerely,

Will Smith

➤ Question 4

Introduction

This proposal aims at preparing a detailed program of activities for a group of business people from the foreign trade delegation who will visit our company next month.

Findings

After serious consideration, I have arranged a series of activities for them. Firstly, I will show them around our company, especially some main departments, to show our corporate culture to them. Meanwhile, I would introduce our company's history and culture for the guests. Secondly, some business lectures would be carried out for the purpose of better communication between two sides. These lectures are given by business experts who are invited honorably. I am sure this will have a significant influence on the cooperation in the future.

Recommendations and Conclusion

After the guests visit the company, they had better meet the vice-manager in the second floor conference room. The two parties can talk about how to cope with the problems in the Globalization Era, which will help better understandings between the two parties.

Outside working hours, we can take all the visitors to take a look at Dalian, especially the seaside. On the last evening, a farewell party will be held in honor of these business people. I am sure they may have a wonderful night and will be impressed by our hospitality.

Day 6

TEST 6

PART ONE

➤ Question 1

- The graph below shows the production of phones sets and cellphones in Telecomm Factory from 1998 to 2008.
- Using the information from the graph, write a short **report** describing the general trend.
- Write **120 – 140** words.

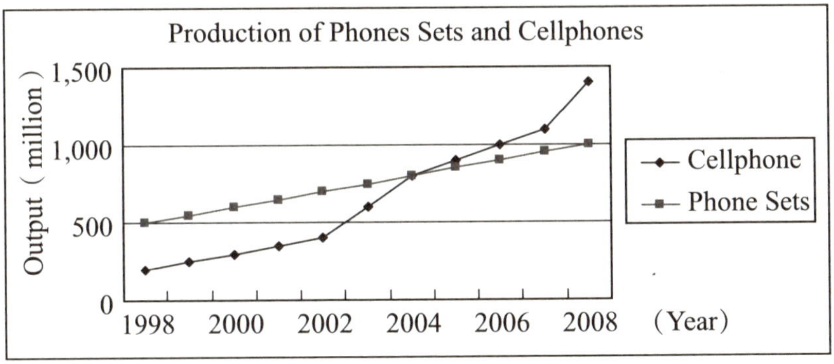

PART TWO

Questions 2 – 4

- Write an answer to **one** of the questions 2 – 4 in this part.
- Write **200 – 250** words on pages 5 and 6.
- Write the question number in the box at the top of page 5.

➤ Question 2

- The Managing Director of your company has decided to cut down costs in your company.
- Write the **report** for your manager, including the following information:
  · Stating the current costs in your company;
  · Suggesting what costs can be cut down;
  · Recommending the possible ways of reducing costs.

➤ Question 3

- Your company has decided to raise the prices of your products which makes a lot of retailers unhappy. Write a retailer a letter to explain it.
- Write the **letter** to the retailer including:
  · Apologizing;
  · Explaining the reasons for raising the prices;
  · Assuring him that it will not affect the sales and telling why.

➤ Question 4

- The Managing Director of your company has decided to better the benefits scheme. You have been asked to put forward a proposal.
- Write your **proposal**, including the following:
  · The employees' attitude towards the current scheme;
  · What new practices could be introduced;
  · Possible dissatisfactions involved in it.

练习参考答案

PART ONE

➤ Question 1

Introduction

This report shows us the production of phones sets and cellphones in Telecomm Factory from 1998 to 2008.

Findings

Although the output of these two products are not steady, we could see the upward trends on the whole. The production of phones sets levels off around 800 million from 1998 to 2001 and then experiences a slight rise to 1,400 million until 2006. Between 2006 and 2008 it remains constant. As for cell phones, the production jumps from 200 million and reaches the peak of 1,400 million in 2005, and then back to 1,100 million in 2006. After that it goes up to 1,200 million in 2007 and declines to 1,100 again in 2007. As we can see, compared with the production of phones sets, the cell phones fluctuates a bit.

PART TWO

➤ Question 2

To: Roger Brown
From: Will Smith
Date: Oct. 23, 2009
Subject: Cost Reduction

Introduction

This report aims to suggest ways of cost reduction.

Findings

We did all right for last year and the first 3 quarters this year, however, the market trend shows that the next couple of years will witness a down-turn in the market. It will be winter for the industry. In such a situation, we will need to develop new channels in terms of marketing, and in the meanwhile look at our current cost and see if we can better it. The current cost is at the market average, and it is not so competitive compared with our major competitors.

Looking at our balance sheet, you will find out that we are comparatively high in terms of G&A cost which includes overhead, administration, and operation cost, new project, and also research and development. This is not a problem if our market goes for the better, as new projects and R&D will improve our productivity and market share. It is also for the same reason that we plan a big number of recruits for next year, and this increases our G&A cost.

Recommendations

In order to sustain our development in the down-turn market, I recommend that we delay our new project, as it will create troubles for us to market it, and the market can even go worse because of increment in supply. For R&D, I recommend that we go on with it, as the investment will result in new products or services, that may possibly get us a better position when the market is up.

➤ Question 3

Dear Mr. Green,

Thank you for your letter concerning the price rise of our products. I deeply regret that it has caused you a lot of inconvenience and I hope that it will soon be steered right.

I think that you understand that during the last two months the price of steel and iron has experienced a steep rise and it naturally leads to the rise of the price of our products. Do you remember that last year the price of raw materials fell and we immediately reduced the prices of our products. In fact the price of our products now is not as high as they were before last year's price change. Furthermore, recently a lot of companies have raised the prices of their products, and their price rise is much steeper than ours.

Now the steel and iron products are in large demand and a large proportion of our workers have to work overtime. However, our supply still does not meet the demand of the market. One of the reasons is that our products have enjoyed high fame worldwide. Given the present wholesale price, I think that our prices still enjoy an advantage and I am sure that you will not feel any pressure on the retail market.

Thank you again for your support which guides us through so many years of our cooperation.

Yours Sincerely,

Will Smith

➤ Question 4

Introduction

The aim of this proposal is to discuss the limitation of the current benefits scheme and how to better it.

Findings

Recently we have conducted thorough interviews among the staff and found that the staff are not very satisfied with our current benefits scheme. On the whole the staff find that it is not flexible enough and hope that a change can be made.

Recommendations

Considering the current dissatisfaction and difficulty, I recommend several practices should be taken accordingly. Our company has always advocated the benefits package. We can not only give the employees bonus and gifts on every festival, but also give out year-end bonus according to his or her performance over the whole year. Furthermore, every employee should be given the chance to travel with the family on the company's expenses. Besides, to those who make great contributions to the development of our company, we should provide an apartment for free. All above could be adopted to add to the present benefits scheme.

Conclusion

To most of the employees, the new practices might give them surprises, which means it can provide more practical treatments. But many new practices have something to do with the employee's performance, which makes the staff feel great stressful. In spite of that, our benefits scheme would bring a change and the staff may feel happy about having something new.

Day 7

TEST 7

PART ONE

➤ Question 1

- The bar chart below shows the number of complaints made by consumers about different types of products and services in the years 2001 and 2007.
- Using the information from the bar chart, write a short **report** describing the changes that took place between 2001 and 2007.
- Write **120 – 140** words.

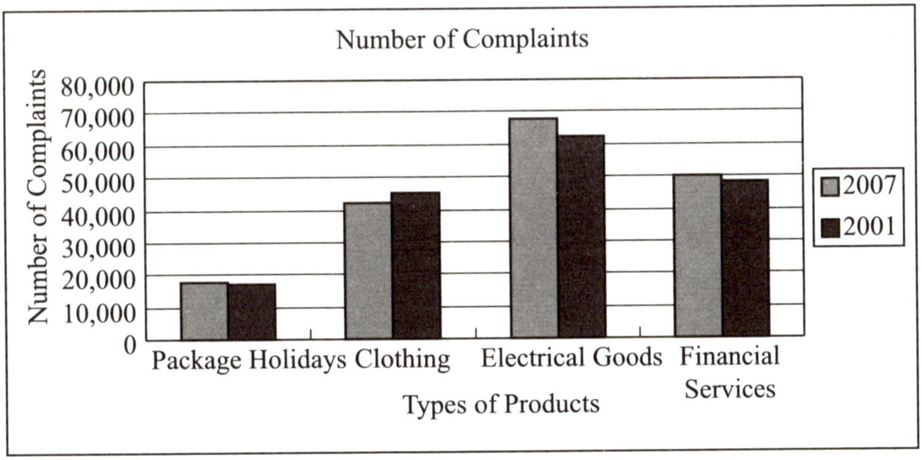

PART TWO

Questions 2 – 4

- Write an answer to **one** of the questions 2 – 4 in this part.
- Write **200 – 250** words on pages 5 and 6.
- Write the question number in the box at the top of page 5.

➤ Question 2

- You are working in an international corporation. Your manager is concerned with the cultural differences in the international environment and has asked you to do some research in the company.
- Write the **report** for your manager, including the following information:
  - · The current situation of communication between staff from different cultures;
  - · Explaining possible causes of misunderstanding;
  - · Recommending ways of improving communication skills between staff of different cultural backgrounds.

➤ Question 3

- The image of your company has gone down recently. A lot of your business partners have come to give you bad evaluation. Write your partners a letter to explain the deterioration of the image of your company.
- Write the **letter** to your business partners including:
  - · Explaining why the image of your company was damaged;
  - · Stating measures to be taken by your company;
  - · Assuring them that your company is always trustworthy.

➤ Question 4

- Due to the economic recession, your company has decided to reduce staff. You have been asked to put forward a proposal concerning this.
- Write your **proposal**, including the following:
  - · Which group of people should be removed first;
  - · Compensation given to the person discharged;
  - · Steps to follow in the reduction.

练习参考答案

PART ONE

➤ Question 1

Introduction

The chart shows the number of complaints made by consumers about different types of products and services in the years 2001 and 2007.

Findings

Focusing our attention on these four aspects it can be seen from the chart that electrical goods get the most complaints and package holidays the least in 2001 and 2007. Over these three years period the number of complaints on package holidays, electrical goods and financial services respectively decreases from 18, 000 to 15, 000, from 68, 000 to 62, 000, and from 50, 000 to 48, 000. In contrast, the number of complaints on clothing has risen slightly from 42, 000 to 45, 000.

PART TWO

➤ Question 2

To: Roger Brown
From: Will Smith
Date: Oct. 23, 2009
Subject: Cultural Differences in Communication

Introduction

This report aims at recommending ways for improving communication skills between staff of different cultural backgrounds.

Findings

As a multinational corporation, we are employing people from 16 countries and areas. We have over 180 expatriate employees, and they comprise 10% of our total employees. The more than 180 people all work as executives, managers, technical experts, and consultants. The expatriate people gave the feedback that sometimes they find the people they lead not able to understand them, and the local people's view is that expatriate people are hard to approach.

Certainly there is misunderstanding between them due to the reason that they are brought up in different cultures. For example, expatriate people prefer to have consensus before they want their subordinates to conduct any action, and that is why they will ask their people for their viewpoints, comments, and concerns; however, local people are good at execution, and they are not used to giving people feedback openly, especially to their bosses. Furthermore, expatriate bosses trust their people's professionalism, and will not check on them regularly; however, local people will think that my boss are not concerned with what they are doing.

Recommendations and Conclusion

We could say that they are both doing the right thing, and what they will need to do more is to know how the other party are thinking, and endeavor to clear misunderstandings. As a result, we will take actions to organize a cross-cultural training course.

➤ Question 3

Dear Mr. Green,

Thank you for your letter concerning how people are talking about the reputation of our company. We also hear about it, yet we did not know exactly how it came. After receiving your letter, we conducted a thorough investigation and have found that in actuality the products of inferior quality were not coming out from our company. They are fake things produced by some small factories and put in similar packs.

Up to now we have collected some of those products and designed a display to show the difference. It is now on show in our main building entrance hall and you can see it any time you come. More than that, we will have a TV reporter arrange an interview with us and we will tell the public about the truth. We sincerely hope that these measures will help clear the fog in our mind. Since we have a long history of cooperation and we know each other very much. When our corporate image is being rubbished, I hope you can support us and see us through. You have told us that we are trustworthy as your business partner and it will prove that we will be as trustworthy as ever.

Thank you very much for the support you have given us.

Yours Sincerely,

Will Smith

➤ Question 4

Introduction

The purpose of this proposal is to discuss how to cope with the problem of overstaff caused by the economic recession.

Findings

Recently, I have carried out a detailed investigation into each employee's performance at work. It is such a pity that I find there is so large a group of people who have no passion for his or her work! As we know, the staff's passion is the soul of our company's development. Those people have gotten used to loafing the day away and have no motivation for work at all.

Recommendations

I think some of the staff in production should be removed as we do not have so big orders as before. Even if there is a large order, the workers could work overtime as they can be better for overworking. As for those who have to leave the company, we can give them one more month's pay as compensation. Although we have to take out some money, we do not have to continue to pay insurances for them. The difference in expenses means that we are saving a lot.

Conclusion

Before reducing the staff, I have investigated each employee's performance and made a proper decision about who to be removed first. And the evaluation of their performance and the calculation of their compensation prove that removing them can help our company out of the difficult situation.

主要参考文献

1.《新版剑桥 BEC 考试真题集》(第 1 辑),商务印书馆 2015 年版。

2.《新版剑桥 BEC 考试真题集》(第 2 辑),商务印书馆 2015 年版。

3.《新版剑桥 BEC 考试真题集》(第 3 辑),商务印书馆 2015 年版。

4.《新版剑桥 BEC 考试真题集》(第 4 辑),商务印书馆 2015 年版。

5.《新版剑桥 BEC 考试真题集》(第 5 辑),商务印书馆 2015 年版。

6.《新编剑桥商务英语学生用书》(高级)(第二版),经济科学出版社 2002 年版。

7.《新编剑桥商务英语教师用书》(高级)(第二版),经济科学出版社 2002 年版。

8.《新编剑桥商务英语同步辅导》(高级),经济科学出版社 2004 年版。

9.《新编剑桥商务英语考试手册 Pass BEC》(中高级),经济科学出版社 2004 年版。

10.《剑桥商务英语证书模拟试题册》(高级),人民邮电出版社 2004 年版。

11.《剑桥商务英语证书考试高分全攻略》(高级),经济科学出版社 2005 年版。

12.《剑桥商务英语写作教程》,北京大学出版社 2000 年版。

13.《剑桥商务英语写作教程》,世界图书出版公司 2006 年版。

14.《剑桥商务英语(BEC)证书考试辅导丛书:高级写作指南》,南方出版社 2004 年版。

15.《剑桥商务英语高级写作应试指南》,人民邮电出版社 2007 年版。

16.《"三最"新编剑桥商务英语》(高级),同济大学出版社 2006 年版。

17. 《挑战 BEC3》（剑桥商务英语高级），国防工业出版社 2005 年版。

18. BEC Handbook for teachers.

19. ALTE（the Association of Language Testers in Europe）官网：https：//alte. wildapricot. org/.